STUDENT IT SKILLS

MARK PETTIGREW

and

DAVID ELLIOTT

Learning and Teaching Institute

Sheffield Hallam University

Gower

Published by
Gower Publishing Limited
Gower House
Croft Road
Aldershot
Hampshire GU11 3HR
England

Gower
Old Post Road
Brookfield
Vermont 05036
USA

Mark Pettigrew and David Elliott have asserted their right under the Copyright, Designs and Patents Act 1988 to be identified as the authors of this work and Peter Hartley, Aileen D Wade and Moira Monteith have asserted their right to be identified as contributors to this work.

British Library Cataloguing in Publication Data.
A catalogue record for this book is available from the British Library.

ISBN   0 566 08053 2

Printed and bound by MPG Books Ltd. Bodmin, Cornwall.

STUDENT IT SKILLS

CONTENTS

ACKNOWLEDGEMENTS

Writing a book is rarely a solo enterprise. This book is the product of a team of people set up for the purpose by Sheffield Hallam University's Learning and Teaching Institute. The team brought together skills and experience in pedagogy, writing, presentation, evaluation and IT. Crucially it included people who consider themselves to be relative novices when it comes to IT and representatives from a range of Schools and Departments within the University.

It has taken over two years of collective effort to conceive, design, draft, trial, evaluate and re-write these chapters. During that time, team members have also been concentrating on their "day jobs" – teaching, research, encouraging innovation in learning and teaching, supporting and developing IT and information services. The rich interaction between these activities and between the team members shows in the breadth of the finished product.

Every member of the team made a substantial contribution to the ideas, structure and content of the book, in addition to the following specific contributions :

Rosie Bingham	trials, evaluation, proofreading, editing
Sue Drew	chair of the group, co-ordination, proofreading, editing
Peter Hartley	co-writing the chapter on layout and style
Moira Monteith	co-writing the chapter on file management, introduction
Aileen Wade	co-writing the chapter on information retrieval
Mark Pettigrew *and*	
David Elliott	the majority of the writing

In addition, Andy Pettigrew co-wrote the File Management chapter.

Thanks are also due to the students and staff of Sheffield Hallam University who acted as guinea pigs for the materials in development and gave us their opinions and advice.

Many of the images in the book have been taken from actual computer programs or Internet web sites. Acknowledgement is given to the rights of the copyright and trademark owners of these programs and web sites.

DE, MP
November 1997

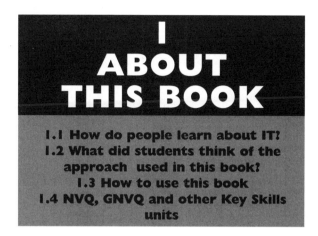

1
ABOUT THIS BOOK

1.1 How do people learn about IT?
1.2 What did students think of the approach used in this book?
1.3 How to use this book
1.4 NVQ, GNVQ and other Key Skills units

1.1 How do people learn about IT?

Most IT training materials are based on following sequences of mouse clicks and keypresses in order to learn how to use a particular program. This approach ignores a number of ideas, strongly grounded in theory, about how you can learn effectively:

- **in order to learn and to use what you have learnt, you need to mentally organise your thoughts and feelings into categories**
- **to learn about IT you need to develop such categories in your mind in which to place what you have learnt; you could see this as understanding principles or constructing a framework on which to build your new learning**
- **you need to reflect on your past experience and knowledge and on your new learning in order to sort your experiences into helpful categories and understand principles**
- **your values and feelings affect your learning**
- **technology changes so quickly that it's more important to learn how to develop IT skills than to learn to use a particular program.**

This book is built on these ideas and on practical experience of helping a wide range of people to learn how to develop IT skills. A team of people from varied backgrounds have contributed to the development of the book, including students who have 'tested' the chapters of this book before the final version was produced.

The book is based on these principles:

- **you need to be flexible, to use a variety of hardware and software. For example, you may use one type of computer at college or university, another at work (if you are in employment), and another at home. Any or all of these are likely to change within a few years.**
- **you are unlikely to transfer learning from one application to another if you simply memorise sequences and do not understand the underlying principles**
- **you are likely to quickly forget the sequences you remember unless you use them regularly**
- **memorising sequences is not very interesting**
- **your feelings about IT are relevant and need to be taken into account**

- in order to continue to adapt to new applications, you need to learn ways of learning about IT which work for you, for example exploring and having the confidence to enable you to explore
- there is a need for a range of different and complementary types of IT materials. If you are faced with a short deadline you may have an immediate need for materials which simply tell you what to do, and may be frustrated by materials which suggest exploration. Once the immediate crisis is over you may find it helpful to then refer to materials like this book which help you grasp the principles.

1.2 What did students think of the approach used in this book?

We evaluated the drafts of this book with a range of students at Sheffield Hallam University. Some of their thoughts are set out here.

Exploration. There were many positive comments about the encouragement of exploration, although not all students liked the approach – a few just wanted to be told what to do.

"I found it helpful to explore, rather than following a prescribed set of instructions."
"It's better to try to find out for yourself."
"Doing it myself meant I learnt more."
"It was fun exploring."
"I prefer to understand what I'm doing."
"Exploring and having to find out yourself gave you more confidence."
"A welcome change from most of the documents we've had so far – they just tell you what to do with few explanations."
"At least there wasn't just a string of instructions!"
"It sort of encouraged you to have a go."
"Encouraging sort of approach – doesn't make you feel you are a complete failure"
"It gave me confidence to try"
"I didn't really want to understand – just wanted to use the system."

Experience, exploring and practice in using computers.
"Trying things out and seeing what happens when you press things."
"Just more experience."

Self awareness. Being aware both of your own skill level and of what you need is important.
"Getting over the embarrassment of not having a clue."
"Not setting myself impossible targets."

Having confidence. Many of the student comments reveal how important it is to build confidence and to allow for and acknowledge a lack of confidence.
"Not thinking I can damage the computer."
"Not being told you haven't got the brains."
"I need to be sure I'm not being useless."
"Getting over the confidence barrier."

1.3 How to use this book

Have a purpose. The book is divided into chapters, each, apart from the first few, covering a specific task you may wish to carry out using a computer. You'll find it most helpful to use each chapter at a time when you need to carry out that particular task. You'll learn most readily when you can see a clear practical need for learning.

Allow time. Learning to use IT takes time and practice, and employment and courses of study often have tight deadlines and high workloads.
"Time to spend coming to grips with it."
"Not trying to do it all at once."

Learning with other people. Work with someone else to learn if you can. People working together help each other to get the most out of learning, whether they are both at the same level or one has more expertise.
"Working alongside somebody who knows what they are doing."
"Learning with someone else of the same level."

Understand your mistakes. This book helps you to understand what you are doing. You can learn from your mistakes by thinking about what you do and building up your understanding of principles. So it's essential to use a computer alongside the book and to explore the programs you're learning about as you read.

Have other materials too. Most people like the exploratory approach used in this book and find that it helps them to develop understanding but it is important to have a range of materials to meet your needs and to switch between them as necessary.

You may, for example, for a specific task:

*   **look at the relevant chapter here, then**
*   **look at the software manual for your program.**

That way you'll bring your increased awareness of principles to bear on exactly how to work the program.

Or you may wish to approach it the other way around:

*   **look at the software manual for your program, then**
*   **look at the relevant chapter in this book.**

That way your practical experience of using the program will help you to build up your understanding of the principles.

You'll find that as you understand the principles, get used to exploring and build up your confidence, you'll need materials about specific programs less and less.

1.4 NVQ, GNVQ and other Key Skills units

NVQ/GNVQ and other Key Skills units spell out in great detail a wide range of IT skills which you must be able to demonstrate, with evidence, in order to be successful. No traditional IT book can cover this complete range and depth as well as the use of a variety of different word-processors, spreadsheets etc.

The approach that this book takes is completely different. Instead of teaching you an enormous number of specific IT skills using particular packages, it helps you to learn a small number of principles about the use of IT and apply them in a wide range of circumstances. You can develop new IT skills as you need them for new tasks. This makes learning about and using IT easier and gives you more confidence to face new IT situations. Using this book can underpin your learning from traditional materials, teachers or work situations with a base of understanding which makes your learning easier.

2
GETTING HELP AS YOU LEARN

The purpose of this chapter is to assist your learning through the rest of the book by helping you to find support as you explore your computer and its programs.

It aims to help you develop some strategies for dealing with those situations where you can't simply work out for yourself what you need to know. Some of this chapter will probably be useful to people learning about computers at any level.

We suggest that you use this chapter:

- away from the computer
- before you start working through the rest of the book
- as a refresher from time to time as you go through the other chapters
- use the 'notes' column to record your own thoughts and ideas as you go.

When you have completed it, you will be able to:

- keep a notebook as you learn
- use suitable strategies to find help as you learn, including exploring, asking others, using the built-in help system, finding suitable books and guides.

The skills that you develop with the aid of this chapter should help you to learn as you work through the rest of the book.

2.1 Background

One of the principal differences between a beginner and an expert in using computers is how they approach new things. The experts tend to have a much larger range of things they will try in order to find their way towards learning about something new on the computer. What you will do in this chapter is look at some of the ways in which you can approach learning about new things, and in particular ways in which you can find out more.

2.1.1 About you

How do you feel about the following ways of finding out more about computers? Mark yourself with a tick on a scale from Good to Bad:

✔	Good		Neutral		Bad
Asking 'experts'					
Asking someone at about the same level as you					
Helping someone else to learn					
Exploring the computer					
Making mistakes					
Reading books					
Making notes as you go along					
Watching videos					
Attending courses					

Don't worry if you've indicated that you feel bad about some of these – as you work through the book you will become comfortable with more of them.

2.2 Adopting a strategic approach to learning

In most other areas of academic learning, the most successful learners usually make notes as they learn. You may be attending a seminar, or reading a book, or watching a video, but the notes you make help you learn in two important ways:

- **it appears that the actual process of writing the information down helps you to fix what you have learnt in your memory**

- the notes are available for you to look over to refresh your memory, either fairly soon after you have made them to help fix what you have learnt in long-term memory, or at a later date when you are looking again for solutions to a problem. Very often, reviewing your notes later helps you to identify patterns in what is going on.

In addition, the decision to keep a record as you learn puts you into a role of learning actively, and that decision to learn is probably the most useful thing you can do towards achieving IT skills.

So – get yourself a notebook in which you can record things as you learn. Keep it with you as you use the computer, and get into the habit of writing down:

- **details of problems you have met**
- **how you solved a problem**
- **successes as you learn**
- **anything you notice that you need to learn more about**
- **people you can ask for help, with phone numbers if possible**
- **useful sources of information (eg particular books)**
- **useful tips and hints.**

If you have a particularly difficult problem, you should try to write down everything you can about it, so that you have as much information as possible to hand as you try to find a solution.

 A brief warning. In general, it will *not* help your *learning* if you write down detailed sequences of instructions like the following:

> Click on File
> Click on Save As
> Click on the little arrow to the right of the box that says Save as type
> Click on Text File (.txt)
> Click on Options
> Click on Always create backup copy
> Click on OK
> Click on the space to the right of File name
> Type the file name
> Click on OK
> Etc, etc

Remember – you are trying to learn the *general principles* of what you are doing, not simply learn a sequence of actions. By and large, computer experts do not simply remember the details of individual sequences – there are far too many of them and there are too many details to learn.

NOTES

Some people keep these notes on the computer; however, you might find it easier to start with a written record. You could use this notes column for your own thoughts and ideas.

If you do find a situation where you think it will be useful to write a sequence of keypresses consider writing a commentary beside it explaining the principles.

What you *are* trying to do is to learn an approach to understanding the computer which will enable you to find your way through any of these sequences for yourself.

It might be more useful to write down things like:

> Save / Save As - on File Menu
>   - Remember 'Options'
>
> **DON'T** put spaces in file names
>
> Remember to **SAVE** before exiting the program!!!!!

2.2.1 Learning from your mistakes

In most (maybe all) areas of learning, you can expect to make mistakes as you learn. Part of the process of learning involves building up your own internal 'picture' or concept of how a system works, and you make mistakes as you improve this picture.

One model of learning describes four processes of learning as follows

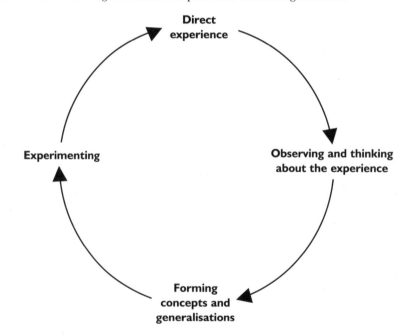

As you learn about computers, it is *necessary* to experiment, to try out your model of what you are learning in order to gain experience and improve your picture of how the computer works. That model will form the basis of your understanding of the computer.

So – you need to adopt a friendly attitude towards mistakes as you learn:

NOTES

- you *will* make mistakes
- you can learn from your mistakes if you make a note of what you did, what happened, and what you have found out as a result.

But – you should try to set aside time to learn when you can make mistakes without causing problems for yourself or others. Don't, for example, try to learn something new and complex by experimenting on an important piece of work with a close deadline.

2.3 Explore

If you watch a computer expert learning to use a new computer program, or learning to use an entirely new computer system, you will see that one of the main things that they do is to *explore*. They let their curiosity take over, and they simply wander round the computer program trying to do things that might help them to understand how the program works.

Throughout this book you will be encouraged to explore. This is a strategy you can adopt in several ways:

- to find out new things that you didn't even know you were looking for – for example, simply looking at things in the program, and trying to figure out what they are for
- to solve a particular problem – for example, you might look round the computer program in order to find something that allows you to print what you have done on paper
- to compare what you already know with something new – so for example, you might explore a new word processor to see if the things that you used on your old word processor are also available on the new one.

NOTES

The first part of exploring a computer program is to simply look at what you can see on the screen. If you look around the computer screen you can often work out what many of the various things you can see are for, even if you have never used a computer program before. As an example, look at this part of a computer screen for a computer drawing program and answer the question which follows:

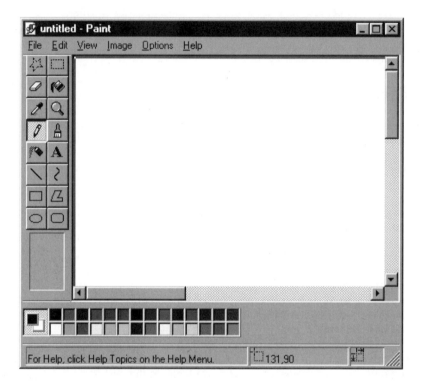

How can you get help on using this program?

The following symbols are 'buttons' (on the left hand side of the picture of the program) which allow you to do things related to drawing. For each one, write a word or two to describe what you think it might do. (Don't worry too much about whether you are actually correct – the important thing is to make a reasonable guess.)

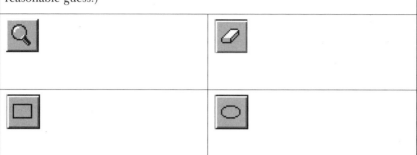

NOTES

As you gather more experience in using a program like this, your guesses will become more accurate.

The next step in exploring is to try things out. As you work through the rest of the book, you will be encouraged to experiment and explore. In many situations, exploring will be a lot quicker than trying to find the answer to a question by asking someone or looking something up, but as you gather experience you will find yourself better at judging what is the most appropriate way of finding out what you need to know.

2.3.1 Investigate

A step up from exploring is investigating. This means trying to find out all you need to know about a particular problem in order to solve it. Useful strategies when you are investigating include:

Make notes relating to the problem

For example, if you are trying to work out how to do something:

- **what exactly are you trying to do?**
- **what else is it similar to?**
- **what words might you use to describe what you want to do?**
- **is there another way you could achieve a similar result?**

If something went wrong:

- **what exactly has gone wrong?**
- **when did it occur?**
- **what were you doing just before the problem?**
- **what have you tried to do to fix the problem, and what happened?**
- **has this happened before? If so when?**
- **can you identify any patterns in what has gone wrong?**

Try to reproduce the problem:

- can you make the same thing happen again?
- what are the common features of all the times you get the problem to occur?

If you can reproduce a problem, it will be very much easier to get someone to help, because you can show them what is happening. If the problem has only occurred once, then it will often be much harder to solve.

Very often, in trying to reproduce a problem you may actually find a solution, either because the thought processes you go through in reproducing the problem lead you to work out a solution, or because as you are exploring the computer to reproduce the problem you stumble across the solution.

Know what sort of solution you require

- Sometimes you simply want the problem to be fixed, and you either don't have time, or else don't care, how it is fixed. For example, you have a piece of work to be finished in an hour and the printer seems to have stopped working; you may need a solution which doesn't require you to spend much time now learning how to fix this problem.

- At other times, what you want is to learn more about the computer, and are less worried about getting a rapid solution. For example, you might want to put a picture into a piece of written work, and because you're likely to want to do this reasonably often you might think it worth spending the time learning how to do it.

Often you can develop an understanding of what has gone wrong, or where the difficulty lies; at other times you may have to accept that you may never (or at least, not for the time being) get to a complete understanding of the problem.

2.4 Get help from others

Remember that asking for help:

- is an important part of learning
- is an efficient way of finding out about something
- shows that you are thinking intelligently about your own progress.

It is **NOT**:

- a sign of failure
- a sign of weakness
- a sign of stupidity.

The following sources of help will prove useful as you learn.

IT support services and helplines	Make a note of the opening times, phone numbers and email address for IT support services. You may be able to get support from: • **within your organisation** • **the people who sold you the computer** • **the manufacturers of the computer programs you use**
Ask someone	Whom could you ask? Write the names of: • **a friend or colleague who knows more about this than you:** • **a teacher or 'expert' who could be useful:** • **a friend or colleague who is at about the same level as you and who would be willing to help:**
Learn with someone	See if you can find someone who is at about the same stage of learning as you, and with whom you could work.

A common experience amongst people learning is that one of the most effective ways of really understanding is to help someone else. So you should consider offering to help someone else use or learn to use the computer. Even if you don't know more about the system than the person you are helping, "two brains are better than one".

2.5 Use the Help system built into the program

Most computer programs come with a reasonably comprehensive 'Help' facility, in which you can use the computer itself to look up information about using the program. (For example, look at the program shown on page 10.) There is more on using the built-in help system in Chapter 3 – **Beginning to Use a Computer.**

In most Help systems, you will be able to type in words to look up, and this will mean developing a reasonable vocabulary of computer terms. As you learn, use your notebook to record any technical terms that you might want to remember.

There is an increasing tendency to provide a good Help system with a computer program rather than to provide written manuals.

2.6 "If all else fails, read the manual"

Depending on your own ways of learning, you may find it useful to look at books and guides to your program:

- **before you start using it**
- **as you learn to use it**
- **when you have a problem.**

There is a very wide range of books, manuals, and guides available for most of the main programs you will use. These include:

- **original manuals – the books that come with the program or the computer, written by the manufacturers. Some of these are very good, and others are less useful**
- **books and videos produced by other people – there is a huge range of computer books and videos available, covering most topics and most programs. Once you have had a chance to start learning about your computer and its programs, it may be useful to spend some time looking in bookshops and libraries to see which ones suit your own style of learning and seem appropriate to the level you are at and the things you want to do**
- **guides – if you are learning in a college or university, or attending a course on a particular program, then the organisation is likely to have written one or more guides to help you use the program. Ask what is available, and look through them to see which you will find useful**
- **computer tutorials – for the most popular programs (for example, the main wordprocessors), there are a number of computer programs designed to help you learn. These are usually available from places where they sell computer programs, and your organisation may already have one or more that you could use.**

Books and videos	Browse through bookshops and libraries and make a note here of any books and videos that suit your own approach to learning.
'In-house' guides	Which ones exist which could be useful to you?
Computer tutorials	Make a note of any that you could find useful

2.7 Reflecting on your progress

Each chapter in this book has a section like this, which will both help you to identify what you should have learnt and serve as a reminder of the main points of the chapter.

✔	Tick what you have done so far.
	Started a notebook
	Realised the importance of a strategic approach to your learning
	Decided to explore
	Identified other people to help you in your learning
	Identified books and manuals that may help you in your learning

3
BEGINNING TO USE A COMPUTER

"Information technology is concerned with the handling of information (which may consist of text, numbers, pictures, sound and other signals) and involves creating, collecting, storing, organising, processing, presenting and communicating information in a variety of electronic forms."

[Focus on IT, NCET, 1991: p18.]

This chapter is a basic introduction to IT for those who:

- are complete beginners
- have a little experience and need a refresher course
- would like to build up confidence.

It aims to help you begin to understand and use computers and information technology. Even if you already understand the basics of using a computer, it may be worth looking through this chapter, as it may help you to learn more about approaching the process of learning about computers and computer programs.

We suggest that you use this chapter:

- to identify what you need to know and want to be able to do
- to discover what method of learning about IT works best for you
- alongside other introductory documents; for example, these may be specific for your computer or for particular programs.

When you have completed it, you will be able to:

- identify your own assumptions and attitudes to IT and how these might influence your learning
- identify ways in which you could use the computer to aid your studies
- identify effective ways for you to learn IT skills eg by exploring
- acknowledge the usefulness of learning from mistakes and identify such learning
- identify and use appropriate sources of help
- identify the general principles of using computer systems
- use common features of the operating environment: mouse; cursor keys; escape key; interpreting the screen
- get the computer to a state where you can start an application
- choose an application
- take appropriate action to cope with the unexpected or with things going wrong
- save your work
- close an application
- monitor your own progress, identify successes and, where you need to, improve.

You should be able to use these skills with any computer system that you may meet, now or in the future, and with any new computer program that you need to use. What you have learnt will be applicable to any task you undertake.

3.1 Your own approach to IT

You can read and think about this section away from the computer.

3.1.1 Your own attitudes and assumptions

You may have assumptions about IT and it may help you to identify these, as our attitudes and assumptions may influence our approach to a new subject. In the following table, read the statement in the first column and tick if you agree with it. Then read the final comments column which contains assumptions which might differ from your own.

Your attitudes and assumptions about IT	Agree?	Comments
IT is difficult to learn		Everyone can reach a useful level of skill
You must be able to type to use a computer		It can help, but is not essential
It's easier for younger people to learn IT		There is no evidence for this
You already know all you need to know about IT		If you do now, you may not in six months' time. Technology changes quickly
Men are better than women at using technology		Some men may be more confident, but everyone uses technology, eg washing machine, car, camera
You must be good at maths and programming to use computers		You don't require maths or programming knowledge to use a computer
IT is only of use for technical areas and subjects (eg Science, Engineering)		All subjects make use of IT eg word-processing an assignment
IT is time-consuming		Yes, it may be, especially as you learn to use it more, but if you use it appropriately, it can save you time
Using a computer is quicker than traditional working methods		This may depend on what you use it for
IT will be more of a help than a hindrance		Yes, it will. There are some things you can't do without it, eg using a modern library catalogue.

3.2 What computers can do

You can read and think about this section away from the computer.

The following lists some of the practical things you can do with a computer. Which could be useful in your work or studies?

Activity	✔
Word process your work	
Add a graph or chart to your work	
Create a table of information	
Do mathematical calculations and analysis	
Include a drawing in your work	
Produce visual aids (slides) for a presentation	
Produce a poster	
Search for material held in the library	
Find information related to your subject	
Communicate with others working in your field	
Use catalogues and other information	
Design and use graphics	
Can you think of any other immediate uses? (List them here)	

Computers process information (also called data). When you use a computer:

- **you give it information (eg words, numbers, pictures or sounds) or you tell it where to get that information**
- **you tell it what to do with that information**
- **the computer does something with the information (eg it converts a set of numbers into a graph)**
- **it produces some sort of output (eg a sound, a picture on the screen, or a printed page of text or numbers).**

The computer can also store and retrieve the information it has been given, so that you can come back at a later date and look at it again or carry on where you left off.

3.3 Learning about IT

You can read and think about this section away from the computer.

3.3.1 Your own approach to learning

How do you normally learn about new things? Do you do any of these?

Approaches to learning	✔
Read course notes/textbooks	
Watch videos/TV	
Make notes as you read, watch, listen	
Focus on what looks easy	
Focus on new challenges	
Trial and error	
Ask a friend to help	
Ask an 'expert' (technical support person / teacher / supervisor / tutor / someone else) to help	
Study with a friend	
Other	

3.3.2 Implications of your current approaches to learning about IT

Listed below are some strategies for learning about IT. When you learned to use a new piece of equipment (e.g. a video recorder) or had to cope with the unexpected from a machine (e.g. your car headlights wouldn't work), which strategies worked best for you?

Link them with your **Approaches to learning** list (above). Could any approaches to learning, different from your usual ones, be effective with IT? What are the advantages and disadvantages of each approach? For example, if you rely on asking someone to show you how to use a video recorder, what if you wanted to record a film but were on your own?

NOTES

On-line
*Information
you can gain
access to
while the
computer is
switched on.
This is
displayed on
the screen.*

Strategy	Advantages	Disadvantages
Refer to the user manuals		
Use quick reference guides		
Watch a training video		
Ask a friend to help you		
Ask an 'expert' to help		
Contact the supplier/manufacturer		
Trial and error		
Apply prior knowledge of a similar situation or piece of equipment to see if it works		
Make notes on what you've learned		
Others		

Two common approaches to learning which are specific to IT are On-line Tutorials and On-line Help.

On-line tutorial
Examples and demonstrations which teach you to do certain tasks by taking you through the stages step-by-step. This allows you to try them out yourself.

On-line help
Information on how to do something, usually accessed by pressing a button or key. This information is often text on the screen.

3.3.3 Learning from mistakes

You are likely to make mistakes with IT. This is an important part of learning, and indicates that you are pushing yourself enough to get into unfamiliar territory.

Mistakes on the computer may not be your fault; computers occasionally make mistakes, they and their software are complex and are never perfect.

Don't be discouraged by mistakes, but make sure that you learn from them. One approach which can help you do this is to:

- **suggest what approaches you could try to solve the problem**
- **try one or more of these approaches until you fix the problem**
- **record what worked**
- **suggest when would be the worst time to make that mistake again**
- **suggest what you could do to ensure it doesn't happen again.**

As you work through the rest of this book, use these boxes to list any mistakes you make and what you have learnt from them.

Mistake	Things you could try to fix the problem	What worked	The worst time to make this mistake	How can you prevent this happening or minimise the damage?
eg: I switched the machine off and didn't save my work	Switch it back on Ask for help	Switching the machine back on, although I lost about five minutes' work	When I have done a lot of work	Be sure to save my work before switching off. Save frequently

You might find it useful to compare your ideas and experiences with someone else.

NOTES

3.4 Computer programs

You can read and think about this section away from the computer.

The computer contains a number of programs (also called applications), eg a word processing program, a drawing package, or a program which handles numerical data.

Program
*(also called
an
application) –
a computer
tool which you
can choose to
carry out a
particular
type of task –
eg drawing.*

In most cases you can choose from different programs on the same computer. The picture here shows the standard programs for one type of computer set-up; you will find something like this on your own computer screen. This particular computer set-up includes:

- **a word processor (WordPad) – used for text (ie like a sophisticated typewriter)**
- **a drawing program (Paint) – for pictures**
- **a calculator program (Calculator) – for numerical calculations**
- **a facility to send and receive faxes.**

plus several other programs. Don't worry too much about any programs you do not know about – there are always likely to be some on any computer you may use.

The table opposite lists some common types of computer applications. Which might you use and how often? Which programs would you find most useful to learn about first. The last column allows you to identify your priorities.

Application	How often do you expect to use it?	Priority (1, 2, 3)
Word processor		
Drawing program		
Electronic mail (email)		
Calculator		
Spreadsheet *(used to deal with tables of numbers)*		
CAD *(Computer Aided Design, for technical drawings etc)*		
Desktop publishing *(for laying out text and graphics to achieve a high quality document like a magazine)*		
Database *(used to handle large amounts of information)*		

NOTES

There are many different types of on/off switch, and some may be hard to find.

3.5 Getting started

You will find it most useful to work through this section at a computer. You may find it useful to make notes as you work through.

 First, you will need to make sure the computer is turned on. Look round the computer for the on/off switch and turn it on. There may be separate on/off switches for the system unit (ie the box with the 'workings') and the monitor (ie the screen).

> *Warning – the computer may already be turned on, even if it looks off. The tell-tale signs include:*
>
> - **a whirring sound from the cooling fan or a humming noise from the system unit**
> - **lights on the front of the system unit.**
>
> If you think the computer is already turned on, you can try a number of things to 'wake it up':
>
> - **check that the monitor is also turned on**
> - **move the mouse (see section 3.6.2)**
> - **press a key on the keyboard**
>
> If you are still stuck, ask someone nearby for help or find an introductory manual or instruction booklet for your computer.

Make a list here of the computer(s) you use most frequently, and where to find the on/off switches.

Location	Computer	Main Switch	Monitor switch

3.5.1 Switching the computer off

 On many computer systems, particularly more modern systems, it may be important that you do not simply turn the computer off by flicking the switch, but instead go through an orderly 'shut-down' sequence before finally turning the computer off. This is dealt with in more detail later, in Section 3.7.4.

3.6 The keyboard and the mouse

At present, you only need to know four things about the keyboard, and five things about the mouse.

3.6.1 The keyboard

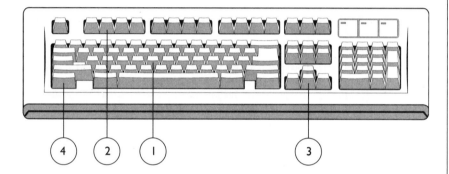

1. Many of the keys on the keyboard act like the keys on a typewriter.

2. Some keys have special functions, which you will learn more about as you work through this book and explore the computer.

3. Some keys help you to move from one part of a piece of work to another.

4. Occasionally you may need to hold down one key and press another at the same time. Examples of these are the shift key (⇧), the control key (Ctrl) and the ALT key and the 'Windows' key on a PC, or the 'Apple' key on a Mac. So, for example, if your instruction manual tells you to press **Ctrl+S**, it means hold down the **Ctrl** key and then press the **S** key. There may be other special key combinations on your computer.

3.6.2 The mouse

It may take some practice to learn to use the mouse smoothly and accurately, but don't worry – it shouldn't take too long.

1. Your mouse works by sliding around on the desk. It may work better on a special mat or a sheet of card, but this is not always essential – sometimes a special mouse mat may even make things worse.

2. On the screen there is a pointer (called a cursor) which you can use to control the computer. To move this cursor, move the mouse around on the desk. The cursor on the screen follows the movement of the mouse.

***'Click on'
something***
*Move the
mouse to
position the
cursor where
you want to
be, press the
mouse button
and then let
go.*

3. You will sometimes need to click the mouse button when the cursor (pointer) on the screen is in a particular position. Your mouse may have one, two or three buttons and each button may have its own function. Because this is specific to each type of computer, you should look at the manual for the computer you are using or ask for help.

4. Sometimes you may need to line the cursor up on something and 'double-click' the mouse button (ie click twice quickly without moving the mouse). This may take a little practice. If this doesn't work as you expected, it may be because you clicked too slowly, or because you moved the mouse in between clicks.

Highlight
*To mark
something on
the screen
(text, part of
a picture etc)
so that you
can do
something
with it (for
example to
delete a
section).*

5. At other times you may be asked to 'drag'. You must first use the mouse to position the pointer on something on the screen and then **hold** down the mouse button and move the mouse. Depending on the application you are using, this may move the object you pointed to around the screen, or else may 'highlight' something on the screen.

3.6.3 Other systems

You may have a different type of pointing device on your computer – for example a trackball or a pointing pad. These are similar to a mouse in that they have:

* **something to move the cursor on the screen**
* **buttons to click.**

You will need to refer to the instruction manual for your own type of pointing device, as they differ in the exact details of how they are used.

3.7 Identifying yourself to the computer

If you are the only person who uses your computer, and it does not ask you for a user name and password when you start it up, then you may be able to skip most of this section for the time being. However, you may need to refer to it again later if you start using a system (for example, an Internet connection) where you do need to use a password.

 Make sure that you do look at the final part of this section, 3.7.4, to find out more about turning your computer off safely.

3.7.1 Logging in to the computer system

When you start using the computer, it may ask you to 'log in' with a 'user name' (or 'User ID') and password. Not all computers will require this – in general, home computers usually do not ask you to log in, and computers connected to a network usually do (for example in larger organisations like companies and colleges).

Welcome to Windows

Type a user name and password to log on to Windows.

User name: BSHAH

Password: ********

OK

Cancel

When you log in with your user name it tells the computer who you are; it may not be the same as your real name. The password is a way of making sure you really are that person – like the PIN (Personal Identification Number) used with a bank cash machine.

You should already have a user name and password for your computer system. If the computer doesn't ask you for a user name, you probably don't need one. If you do not have a user name and password, and the computer does ask for one, you will need to find out how to get them. Whoever is responsible for setting up your computer should be able to help you.

NOTES

*A **network** is a way of connecting computers and other equipment like printers together. A printer can thus be shared between several computers, and people working on different computers may be able to pass information to one another.*

When you type in a password, it will usually not appear on the screen; you may see asterisks, or you may see nothing as you type.

Typing in your user name and password is called 'logging in'.

Log in using your own user name and password

To get into the computer, log in with your user name and password. You will see some sort of log-in screen asking for this information, often when you first start using the computer.

You can usually type your user name straight away, but before you can type in your password you will have to do something like:
• press the **Tab** key
• click with the mouse in the password box
• press the **Return** or **Enter** key.

Ask if you are not sure how to do it. No-one minds helping someone to get going, and once you have learnt you can help others.

> *Just like with a bank PIN, your password must be kept secret. It should never be written down. This may not seem important now, but it's a good habit to get into. Secret passwords are vital where confidential or important information is kept, and can help you to ensure that someone doesn't accidentally change your work.*

3.7.2 Changing your password

From time to time the computer may ask you to change your password. This helps to ensure that the computer system is 'secure' – in case passwords become known by the wrong people. If the computer does not ask, it is still usually a good idea to change your password regularly, or when you think someone else may know what it is.

You are usually allowed to make up your own password. Good passwords might be:

- **two unrelated words joined together (eg dogdesk)**
- **a mis-spelt word (eg potayto)**
- **a date plus a letter or two (eg 130695AH) but beware of using your own date of birth**
- **a word with numbers in it (eleph5ant).**

Character
A letter, number or punctuation symbol produced by one of the 'typewriter' keys on your keyboard.

Identify a few passwords to fit the descriptions for each of the columns on the next page. Each password should be at least six characters long. Try to use only combinations of letters and/or numbers without spaces, since many password systems require this.

Passwords that are easy to remember, but also easy for someone to guess if they know you	Passwords that would be hard to remember, but also difficult to guess.	Passwords that are easy for you to remember, but also difficult for someone else to guess.
Don't use these!	Don't use these!	Use these!

NOTES

Try changing your computer password.

The procedures for changing passwords are specific to particular types of machine. You will almost certainly need to ask someone how to do this, or look for instructions in a manual, a support booklet, or on-screen help.

3.7.3 Logging out at the end of a session

If you had to log in to the computer system, you will often need to 'log out' (or 'log off') again at the end of your session. This allows other people to use the computer after you.

Before you log out you should save any work you have done – see page 43.

Log out at the end of a practice session

There are many different ways of logging out from a computer system, and again you will need to find out how to do this for your system. The main points to remember are:

- **you will need to 'exit' from any programs you have been using to avoid losing work**
- **there may be a method of logging out that you should follow, although some systems will log off automatically if you switch the computer off**
- **if there is a proper method of logging out, do not simply switch the computer off instead – this may result in losing work.**

Log out
To tell the
computer that
you have
finished the
session.

3.7.4 Turning off the computer

At some point, you will need to turn off the computer. If you don't want to turn your computer off now, it is still worth reading through this section now to be ready when you do want to finish with the computer.

 Do not turn your computer off *until* you have read through this section.

There are three main ways of turning off a computer:

- **the same switch you used to turn the computer on**
- **by doing something with the computer keyboard or mouse to tell it you want to turn off**
- **some portable computers will switch themselves off automatically after a certain period of time without use.**

With many computers, you must go through some sort of 'shut-down' procedure before you turn it off. This may involve:

- **closing any applications (programs) you are using**
- **using the mouse or the keyboard to choose a 'switch off now' item from a list.**

Because this could be important, you should ask someone or look at the instruction manuals for your computer.

3.8 Using an application

Once you have turned on the computer, and logged into the network if you have one, you can start using the computer.

This section goes through starting up a program, doing something with it (eg typing something into a word processor), printing what you have done, and finishing.

Remember that you are more likely to be successful in what you are trying to do and in what you are trying to learn if you identify and use sources of help. Chapter 2 – **Getting Help as You Learn** gives some suggestions, and it may be a good idea to review that chapter before you go any further.

3.8.1 Choosing an application

The computer has a number of programs that you can use. You will probably be able to see them on the screen when you have the computer turned on and ready to use. On many systems, there will be a symbol for each program, usually with a name underneath or beside it. However, your own computer system may be set up just to give names of programs.

It is often obvious what a program is by its name or its icon, although sometimes it may not be so easy. What would you guess each of these programs and its symbol represents? (Tick in one column for each symbol/name).

Program name	Symbol	Word processor	Spreadsheet (to do with numbers)	Drawing/ painting program
Microsoft Word		✔		
Microsoft Excel				
Lotus 123				
Paintbrush				
Word Perfect				
RightWriter				
Ami Pro				
Corel Draw				
Write				
MacWrite				
SuperPaint				

There are many other types of program.

Use this table to record what type of program you intend to use first. You may find it useful to look back at your answers on page 25. Most students find a word processor useful, and this may be an appropriate program to begin with.

Which type of program have you chosen? (tick one)	Name of the program	Icon	What do you want to be able to do with it?
Word processor			
Spreadsheet			
Drawing program			
Database			
Electronic mail (email)			
Other [specify]			

3.8.2 Starting your chosen application

NOTES

There may be several ways of getting the program going. Some of the most common are:

1. Double click the mouse button on the program icon (see page 28). This may start the program directly.

2. Click on the symbol for the program you want to start. The symbol should change to show that you have selected it. Look at the menu bar at the top of the screen, set the mouse to click on each word in turn (**File, Edit,** etc) until you find an **Open** or **Run** item in the list that drops down below the menu bar. Click on that.

Run / Open / Launch
To start a program.

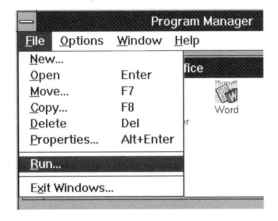

A variation of this method in some computers is to click and hold on a word in the menu bar, drag the mouse down until it hits the Open or Run item in the list, and then let go of the mouse.

3. Click on the symbol for the program you want to start. The symbol should change to show that you have selected it. Then press the Return or Enter key on the keyboard.

NOTES

4. Use the mouse to work through a 'cascading' menu system, choosing from each menu in turn to 'focus in' on your chosen application.

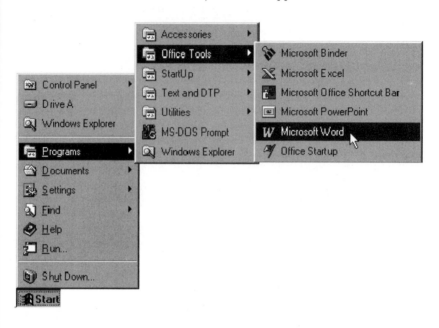

A computer may start up some programs automatically when you turn the computer on, either because it has been set up that way, or else because you left those programs open the last time you used it.

 Try it.

If you try one method and it doesn't work, try one of the others. You should now see the program start up. If not – try again or **ask** for help!

3.8.3 Exploring your chosen application

Now that you have got the program started, one of the best ways to learn how to use a computer program is to experiment with it. Do this **before** you do any important work, in order to avoid losing it as you experiment. You may find it helps to work with someone else at about the same level.

With whom could you co-operate on this?

A good starting point for exploration is to click on things in the program window on the screen to see what they do.

Exploring Menus

Click on each of the words (eg **File, Edit,** etc) in the menu bar at the top of the program window (see below). This will show you a list of words.

You may need to try a different mouse button or hold the mouse button down, depending on your computer.

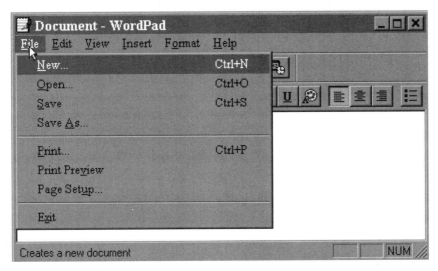

These lists or 'menus' indicate what the computer can do under each heading. Note any that might be useful immediately, and try to predict what they do. Don't worry about the ones you don't understand yet. If you get stuck while you are exploring, look at Section 2.9.

Menu heading	Items which could be useful to you	What each item does
File	Open Save Print	

NOTES

Window
A box on the screen showing what is happening in one program or part of a program.

Menu
A list of things you can choose to do.

NOTES

Exploring Buttons

Most programs have one or more rows of 'buttons' with text and/or pictures on them to help you to do things in the program. These are often called toolbars.

Explore by clicking on the buttons in the program (little pictures at the top or side of the window area).

In many programs there is a way of seeing what each button does. Try the methods below (one or more may work with your system):

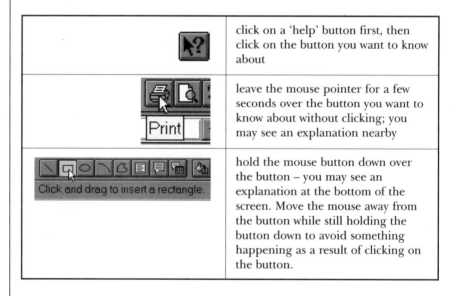

	click on a 'help' button first, then click on the button you want to know about
	leave the mouse pointer for a few seconds over the button you want to know about without clicking; you may see an explanation nearby
	hold the mouse button down over the button – you may see an explanation at the bottom of the screen. Move the mouse away from the button while still holding the button down to avoid something happening as a result of clicking on the button.

Icons to be wary of when exploring are 'maximize' and 'minimize' buttons (usually at the top right of the screen, although they may not be there at all in some cases). A maximise button will make your work take up the whole of the screen; a minimise button might seem to make your work disappear, but in fact reduces it to a small icon or other representation somewhere on the screen. Clicking on this small icon should give you a clue about how to get your work back to normal size again.

Minimise button   *Maximise button*

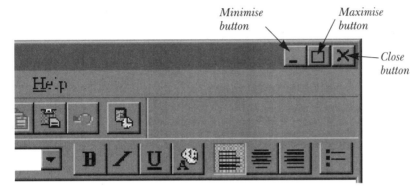

— *Close button*

Watch out for the 'close' button – this will close down the program.

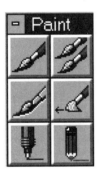
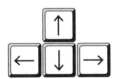

If you are using a word processor, spreadsheet or database, type something to see what happens. As well as typing letters and numbers, you could also try pressing the up, down, right and left arrow keys (called cursor keys), the Enter or Return key, and the Tab key.

If you are using a drawing program, try holding the mouse button down over the drawing area and moving the mouse. You could also try clicking first on some of the drawing tool buttons at the side, top or bottom of the screen. One of these may look like a paintbrush or pencil.

One advantage of computers is that they allow you to move things around in your work. Find and sketch below the buttons that your computer uses to allow you to carry out the following:

Clipboard
A space in the computer where fragments of work are placed temporarily in order to copy or move them somewhere else.

Action	Icon	What it does
Cut		Removes whatever you have selected and puts it into a 'clipboard', ready for you to paste (see below) somewhere else
Copy		Copies whatever you have selected into the clipboard ready for you to paste somewhere else
Paste		Takes whatever is in the clipboard and puts it into your work at the point where you are currently working

3.8.5 Learning from your exploration

As you learn about this new program, it may be helpful to make a list of questions or problems you have, and to record any answers/solutions.

Question/problem	Answer/solution

3.9 When (not 'if') you get stuck!

At some point during your exploration something unexpected may happen, eg you may see a new box on screen with a message in it, or you may see something change that you did not plan to alter.

The following suggests some approaches to solving problems. You can find out exactly how you can use each approach for your own system. You may need to use the help system, read a guide or a manual, or ask someone.

3.9.1 Removing unwanted boxes and windows from the screen

The diagram below shows three common ways of removing unwanted boxes and windows. Your own computer system may look different from this, and may not have all of these possibilities, but the principles will be similar.

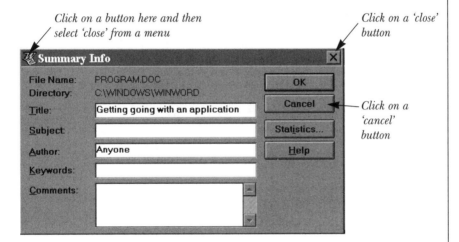

You can also try pressing the Escape key **(Esc)** if there is one. There may be a differently named key or key combination on your computer.

If you get stuck, ask for help before it becomes a serious problem. If you are doing particularly important work on the computer and something goes wrong, then asking for help early may save a lot of effort later on.

3.9.2 'Undoing' something

Most programs can 'undo' what you have most recently done. You may see a button for this, or try clicking on the menu bar items until you find an undo item. There may be a shortcut key for 'undo'; eg in the program shown here the **Undo** item is on the **Edit** menu, and has the shortcut key combination **Ctrl+Z** (hold down the key marked **Ctrl,** and then press **Z**).

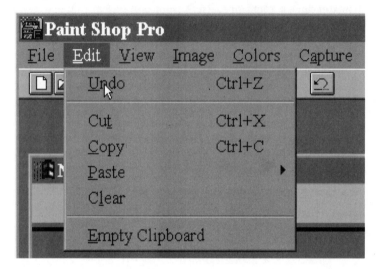

Try typing in some text, and then use the undo facility. Did it work as you expected? Sometimes it may remove more or less than you wanted.

Make a note here of the location of your own program's **Undo** menu item, its key combination and what button (if any) you can use instead. You will probably need to use these often.

Menu containing Undo	Key combination	Button

3.10 'Saving' your work

Every time you have done a few minutes' worth of work, you should 'save' what you have done. If you don't save your work before you finish your session at the computer, then you will have to start again from the beginning next time.

In this section you will learn about using floppy disks and how to save your work. Chapter 12 – **File Management** – covers this in more detail

3.10.1 Using 'floppy disks'

In many cases, you will probably save your work onto a 'floppy disk'.

Although modern floppy disks are fairly robust, they need to be treated with care. Just like a video or audio cassette, they can be damaged by

- **high temperatures (eg in a car window in bright sunlight)**
- **magnetic fields (eg near a magnet, a telephone or a loudspeaker)**
- **dust (eg in a pocket or a rucksack)**
- **water and grease.**

Insert the disk fully into the slot on the front of the computer, metal edge first, until it clicks into place.

Before you can use a floppy disk it must have been 'formatted'. The disks you buy will usually **not** have been formatted (although some are).

Find out how to format a floppy disk for your computer. Again, you may need to ask, or look for help in a manual or on the help system for your computer.

> Note the way you format a floppy disk for your computer. The first disk you format may last you a while, but at some point you may have to format another.

NOTES

Save
To transfer the work you have done from the computer's short-term memory into its long-term storage (such as a floppy disk) so that you can return to it at a later date.

Formatting (also called initialising a disk)
Preparing a disk to hold information. This is usually done by the computer you are working on.

NOTES

3.10.2 Saving your work

The way you save your work may vary between computers, but for any one computer system it is likely to be standard for the applications you use. Look for these three methods:

Where a menu incudes both **Save** *and* **Save As,** *you can use:*

• **Save As** *to give your work a name or to give it a new or different name and then save it*

• **Save** *to save your work with the name it already has*

Method		Specific details for your computer and your program
Use a 'Save' item on one of the menus (probably the 'File' menu)		
Click on a 'Save' button (which will usually include a picture of a disk)		
Use a keyboard short-cut combination, often shown on the menus. This is likely to be one of the special keys plus S.		

The first time you save work, you will usually be asked to give it a name. Choose one which will help you to remember what the work is. Some computer systems restrict your choice of names, eg by:

• **using eight characters or less**
• **using only letters and/or numbers and/or some of the punctuation symbols**
• **forbidding spaces in names.**

If you try to use a name which the computer does not allow, it may ask you to change it or may even change it for you.

3.11 Closing down your application

When you have finished exploring, you must close down the program you are using.

Do not simply turn off the computer. This is bad practice, and you may end up losing work.

 Find the menu item that allows you to exit from the program. You may do this by:

- **looking at the manual or introductory guide for the program**
- **looking in the program's help system**
- **exploring the menus by clicking on each item in turn**
- **asking someone.**

Note: there are several words for this – **Exit, Quit** *or* **Close. Close** *may leave the program open but close down the document/picture/data that you were working on.*

Record the menu item and any short-cut key combination that allows you to exit from the program.

Menu containing exit/quit	short-cut key combination

There may also be a button which allows you to close the program

for example: **X**

 Choose a way of closing the program, and use it.

3.11.1 Warning messages as you close the program

When you close the program, you will often get a message like this:

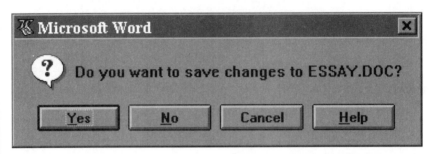

This means that you have done some work on the computer but you have not put your work safely onto a disk. The computer is giving you a choice of how to deal with this.

Read the message carefully, and take some time to think about which button to press, so that you don't make a mistake you regret.

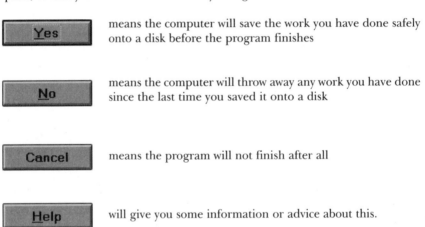

means the computer will save the work you have done safely onto a disk before the program finishes

means the computer will throw away any work you have done since the last time you saved it onto a disk

means the program will not finish after all

will give you some information or advice about this.

On your own system the buttons may use different words, for example **Save, Discard** and **Don't Exit,** but the meaning should be clear.

3.12 Reflecting on your progress

You can complete this section once you have finished at the computer. It may help to look back over your notes to the previous section.

✔ Tick what you have learnt to do so far.
Identify your own attitudes and assumptions about computers
Identify some ways in which computers could help you in your work
Recognise how your own approaches to learning apply to learning about IT
How to learn from mistakes
Turn the computer off safely
Identify the main keys of the keyboard
Use a mouse
Log in and out (if appropriate to your own system)
Change your password (if appropriate to your own system)
Choose a suitable application
Start and close a computer program
Explore a computer program
Save your work
Find ways of dealing with problems

How do you feel now about the prospect of learning more about using computers?

3.12.1 What next?

You may now have some ideas about what you would like to learn to do next. Although the chapters of this book are arranged in an order which means that the least complex chapters come first, you do not necessarily need to go through them in the order that they come in the book. Each chapter has a section at the beginning called *Before you start,* which indicates what you need to be able to do before using that chapter.

The remaining chapters are listed below.

Which of these chapters do you think would be most appropriate for you to look at next? (You might want to look ahead and briefly skim through each chapter to see what it offers). Write a number next to each to indicate its priority for your own learning. This will help you to plan your learning.

Chapter title	Priority
4. Writing	
5. Making tables	
6. Working with numbers	
7. Making charts and graphs	
8. Using electronic mail	
9. Surfing the World Wide Web	
10. Retrieving information	
11. Working with several windows	
12. File management	
13. Layout and style	

Make a note here of any other things you need to do now as you continue to learn about using computers.

4
WRITING

4.1. Background
4.2 At the computer
4.3 Reflecting on your progress
4.4 What next?
4.5 The computer keyboard

This chapter is a basic introduction to using text on a computer.

It aims to help you get started in using a word processor, and will get you to the point where you can produce a simple printed document, such as a short essay. What you learn using this chapter will be useful whenever you produce text on a computer, whatever computer program you use, eg when you use text in other programs such as spreadsheets, databases and graphics packages.

It will **not** teach you to operate a specific make of word processor. Other resources are available to help you with that – eg introductory booklets, manuals – and you may need to refer to these or ask other people for help as you learn.

Before you start:

- you should already know how to start a suitable application such as a word processor
- you should understand the basic features of your computer, eg how to work with windows and a mouse. Chapter 3 – *Beginning to Use a Computer* helps you to get to this point, and will help you with any points you don't already understand in this chapter.

When you have completed this chapter, you will be able to:

- use the keyboard to type in and correct text
- print your work
- highlight text
- change the appearance of words
- identify effective ways for you to learn IT skills
- monitor your own progress, identify successes and where you need to improve.

The skills that you develop with the aid of this chapter should help you to learn to use any word processor. You should also develop further the skills you need to seek help and support from other sources, including manuals, on-line help, other learners and support services.

4.1 Background

You can read and think about this section away from the computer.

4.1.1 What you are going to do

One of the most successful ways to learn to use a computer is to explore. In this Chapter, we help you to *explore* a word processor.

> *Remember that it is best to try to learn the general principles of using the computer, rather than trying to copy down or learn sequences of keypresses.*

4.1.2 Identify a suitable task

People often find it most effective to learn by carrying out a real task at the computer. However, practising on a task which is complex, is large, or must be finished in a short time, may put pressure on you which could prevent you from learning most thoroughly.

Things do go wrong while you are learning to use IT, so you should treat this as a chance to learn rather than a chance to produce an essential piece of work.

A suitable task is likely to involve producing a piece of text:

- **longer than a page, but not much more**
- **with a single heading or a series of similar headings**
- **with no extra features such as pictures, boxes, lines, columns.**

Examples might include:

- **the text for a letter**
- **a couple of pages about yourself**
- **the text for a magazine article**
- **a short essay**
- **an abstract**
- **a short report.**

The finished article is likely to look something like the picture below. However, what you use as a practice task will depend on your own needs.

It may be a good idea to have the text of what you want to produce already written out, so you will not have to practise composing text at the computer at the same time as learning to use the word processor.

Make notes here about your task.

Before you start – reflect on what you might do when things go wrong. If you worked through Chapter 3 – **Beginning to Use a Computer,** you will have identified useful strategies such as:

- trying the **Undo** facility
- asking for help, either from someone nearby, from a knowledgeable friend or colleague, or from a support service
- reading the manual
- using the **Help** facility
- making notes on what went wrong, what you did, and what happened.

4.2 At the computer

You will find it most useful to work through this section at the computer. You may find it useful to make notes as you work through.

4.2.1 Typing something

Start the word processor with a new piece of work. If you are not sure how to do this, you could try:

- exploring
- looking again at **Chapter 3** – Beginning to Use a Computer
- looking at an introductory manual or guide for your word processor
- asking for help.

Now – start typing. To start with, just type in the title, and then press the **Enter** key twice.

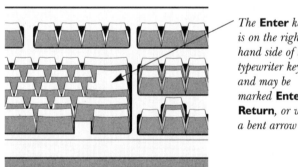

*The **Enter** key is on the right hand side of the typewriter keys, and may be marked **Enter**, **Return**, or with a bent arrow*

The keyboard diagram on page 63 indicates what some of the special typing and editing keys on the keyboard do. It may help to look at this before you proceed and to keep it by you as you work.

You can start typing in the rest of the text you want. Don't worry too much about how the typing looks.

At the end of a line, you can either:

* just keep on typing – the words you type will spill onto the next line when one line is full; this is called **word-wrap**
* or press the **Enter** key – this will force the computer to start a new line.

The usual practice is to use the **Enter** key only at the end of a paragraph, and let the computer use word-wrap to sort out the line ends in the middle of paragraphs.

You will learn later how to make your text look more attractive. For now, however, put an extra line between paragraphs by pressing the **Enter** key twice at the end of a paragraph; this will make your work easier to read.

Correcting typing mistakes

The **Backspace** *key is very useful – to see how it works, try pressing it briefly a few times when you have typed in some text. Section 4.2.2 covers how to correct errors further back without having to retype a lot of work.*

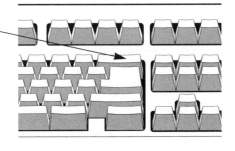

Most computers offer an **Undo** facility. It is probably a good idea to practise using it now so you can find out how it works when you are working with text in your program. To help you explore, you could fill in the following information about **Undo** on your system.

NOTES

How do you **Undo** something on your word processor?

When you have just typed some text in, does using Undo:

delete the last character?
delete the last word?
delete the last sentence?
delete everything you have typed since the last time you did something else?

A note about line breaks:
When you press the **Enter** *key, it puts an invisible mark in the text that tells the computer to start a new line. This mark is treated like any other character (letter, number, space, punctuation mark, etc), and you can erase it using the* **Backspace** *key or the* **Delete** *key.*

If unexpected things happen, make a note of what you did just before the problem. Then you can try:

* pressing an **Escape** key
* looking for an 'opposite' of what you just did (for example, if you pressed a key called **Page Down,** then you could try pressing **Page Up**)
* looking for an option that says **Cancel**
* repeating what you did – this may either cancel what you have done, or else may help you to understand how you made the mistake so you don't do it again
* asking someone for help – this is especially useful if what happened seems very strange to you; you could waste a lot of time trying to work something out when someone else might be able to tell you the answer quickly.

Whatever you do to fix a problem, make a note here (or even a mental note) of what you did, what happened, and how you fixed it.

Now save your work. (If you don't know how, refer to Chapter 3 – **Beginning to Use a Computer**.)

You will need to think of a suitable name (for example *Letter, Essay, Project1, Report*). It is very important to save your work early and often. Each time you save your work from now on, the new version you save will replace the old version on your disk.

As you type more than a screenful of text into the computer, either now or later, you will find that text disappears off the top of the screen – the screen is **scrolling** to allow you to see where what you type is going. The computer is showing you a **window** into your work.

If you want to look further back in a large piece of writing, you can use the scrollbars (usually at the right of where you are writing) to **scroll** this window up and down through your work. There are sometimes slight differences in the way scrollbars work on different computers.

When you have more than a screenful of text typed in, find the scrollbars and explore by doing the following. Make a note of what each does:

1. Click on single arrowheads at the top and bottom of the scroll bar

2. Click above and below the **thumb** on the scroll bar

3. Point the mouse cursor at the **thumb,** and keeping the button held down try **dragging** the thumb up or down to see what happens.

4.2.2 Correcting your work

You should now know how to make corrections at the end of your work using the **Backspace** key. This section helps you make corrections further back in the text.

Find a word to change near the start of your work. Since this is a practice, it doesn't really matter what you change.

You need to tell the computer **where** you want to make the change.

The point in your text where the new text is placed as you type is called the insertion point

Move the mouse so that it is pointing to the start of the text you want to change, and then click the mouse button. *(This is most likely to be the left button if the mouse has more than one button.)*

Move the mouse away and look at the place where you clicked.

Now try typing. What happens?

Keep typing and make a note here of what happens to the ends of any lines further down the text as you type.

Predict what will happen if you move the mouse to a point in the text, click the mouse button, and then press the **Backspace** key.

Try it and see if you were right.

4.2.3 Exploring further

The exercises below help you explore further features of the word processor. We suggest you try to predict the answer in each case, and then try it to see if you were right.

 Try pressing the **Page Up (PgUp)** key and the **Page Down (PgDn).** You will need lots of text to see clearly how these keys work.

What you think will happen	What actually happened?

 Try pressing the up, down, left and right **cursor** (arrow) keys

What you think will happen	What actually happened?

 Try pressing the **Home** and **End** keys

What you think will happen	What actually happened?

NOTES

Some important keys are shown on page 63. If you press the **Tab** *key while you are typing, it will put a space into the text.*

If your keyboard has a key called **Delete,** *it may either delete text you have selected, or else (depending on your computer) may delete the character to the right or left of the insertion point.*

4.2.4 Printing your work

When you have completed a piece of work, or at points where it may be useful to have a paper copy of what you have done so far, you will need to print your document.

 Try printing your work now.

If you don't know how to print, you could try:

- exploring – look for a button that looks like a printer or a **Print** item on a menu and click on it
- looking in a manual for advice on how to print
- asking someone else for help

4.2.5 Changing the appearance of words

Formatting *text means changing the appearance of the text – for example, by making certain words* **bold,** *or changing the layout of the text on the page.*

You may want to change the way some words or letters on the page appear. For example, you may wish to have a heading in **bold** or make certain words be *italic*.

The general approach to formatting parts of your work is to:

- **indicate what text you wish to change**
- **tell the computer how you want it changed.**

 Move the mouse to point to the start of the text you wish to format (A)

Now, *holding down the mouse button,* move the mouse pointer to the end of the text you wish to change (B-C) then release the mouse button (D). This may take some practice.

A ... here is the word you want to change ...

B ... here is the word you want to change ...

C ... here is the word you want to change ...

D ... here is the word you want to change ...

The text you wish to change will now be 'highlighted', or marked to distinguish it from other text. In the example shown here, it has been highlighted in black.

Now you can tell the computer how to change the highlighted text, for example making it bold. There are often a number of different ways of doing something on a computer, even in a single program, and you may need to:

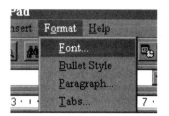

- **click on a bold button on a toolbar**
- **choose something from a menu which allows you to change text to bold**
- **or you may find other ways of doing it which suit the way you like to work.**

If you haven't already experimented with changing text to **bold,** or *italic,* then try changing your heading to **bold,** and select a couple of words in the text to change to *italic*.

> *A note on underlining*
> *Although* **bold** *and italic are common ways of emphasising text,* <u>*underlining*</u> *particular pieces of text is not generally considered a good idea in word-processed documents because it is often not as easy to read.*

  If you have time you could also try the following. Make a note of what happens:

• Highlighting some text and then pressing the **Backspace** key	
• Moving the cursor to the middle of a line and clicking the mouse, and then pressing the **Enter** key	
• Investigating the difference between the **Backspace** key and the **Delete** key, if your computer has one	
• Pointing the cursor in the middle of some text and double-clicking or even triple-clicking the mouse button	
• Moving the cursor to the middle of some text and pressing a different mouse button if your mouse has one	

NOTES

Don't forget the ways you have learnt of getting out of trouble — for example using **Undo** or pressing the **Escape** key.

Remember to save your work, and print it if you want, once you have made all your changes for this session at the computer.

Finally, you should exit from your program, and close down the computer properly. If you don't already know how to do this see Chapter 3 – **Beginning to Use a Computer.**

4.3 Reflecting on your progress

You can complete this section once you have finished at the computer. It may help to look back over your notes to the previous section.

✔	Tick what you have learnt to do so far.
	Type text in
	Start a new line
	Type into the middle of your work
	Delete text
	Save your work
	Print your work
	Use the cursor (arrow) keys
	Use the page keys (Page Up, Page Down)
	Use the Home and End keys
	Select (highlight) a part of the text
	Make selected text bold
	Make selected text italic

How do you feel now about the task you set yourself?

Do you feel you have succeeded in what you tried to do?

If so, what contributed most to the success? If not, what in particular did you find difficult?

If you have identified some aspects of learning to use a computer which you find difficult, you could:

- **talk with someone else who is at about the same level as you but who is not finding those particular things difficult**
- **talk to someone who is more expert than you**
- **contact a support service.**

or you may simply find it useful to take a break and come back another time and have another go.

4.4 What next?

Are you happy with what you have produced?

> As a way of helping you to decide what you want to learn about next, look at a professionally produced word-processed document, such as this book. Are there any features that you would like to learn soon (for example, using different styles of heading, text in boxes etc)?

You may find it useful to learn to type using all your fingers. There are many 'typing tutor' programs and courses available. With practice, you should be able to reach a speed of at least 20 words per minute typing, and possibly much faster. This will help you to produce typed work more quickly and accurately, and will make your time at the computer more enjoyable and much easier in the long run.

4.5 The computer keyboard

This picture shows one of the types of keyboard you may meet. Computer keyboards are generally pretty similar, although some of the details may vary from computer to computer. Some keyboards may not have all of the keys shown here, may have extra keys, or may have some keys in different places.

The special keys you need to know about when you are using the computer for text are marked. You may find it useful to explore the use of these keys to gain a better understanding of how they work on your computer.

Escape key.
May be somewhere else
on the keyboard. This
is often marked **Esc**.

Enter key.
May also be marked
Return or with a
bent arrow

Tab key.
May be marked
Tab or with two
arrows pointing
left and right

Backspace key.
May be marked
with an arrow
pointing to the left

Delete
key

**Page Up, Page
Down, Home,** and
End keys. Used for
moving around in the
document

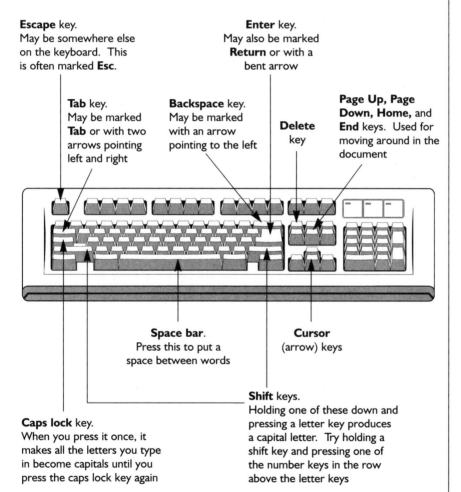

Space bar.
Press this to put a
space between words

Cursor
(arrow) keys

Shift keys.
Holding one of these down and
pressing a letter key produces
a capital letter. Try holding a
shift key and pressing one of
the number keys in the row
above the letter keys

Caps lock key.
When you press it once, it
makes all the letters you type
in become capitals until you
press the caps lock key again

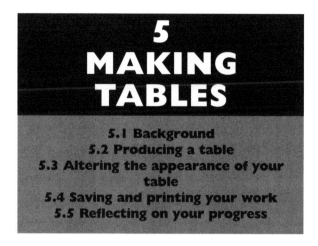

5
MAKING TABLES

5.1 Background
5.2 Producing a table
5.3 Altering the appearance of your table
5.4 Saving and printing your work
5.5 Reflecting on your progress

This chapter is a basic introduction to producing and editing tables of information on a computer.

It aims to help you make tables, using a word processor. The examples and pictures in the text come from different programs and computers, and illustrate the general principles.

If you want to use tables of numbers to do calculations, Chapter 6 – **Working with Numbers** may be more appropriate to your needs at this point.

Before you start:

- **you should know the basics of using a word processor. Chapter 4 – *Writing* will help you to get to this point.**

When you have completed this chapter, you will be able to:

- **identify when it would be useful to make a table using a computer**
- **tell your word processor to make a table with a particular number of columns and rows**
- **put information into a table**
- **change the appearance of a table, eg changing the type style, inserting borders or shading, changing column widths**
- **save and print your work**
- **monitor your own progress, identify successes and where you need to improve.**

What you learn will provide a good foundation for using and learning about tables in any word processor, on any personal computer using a graphical display (for example, running Windows).

NOTES

5.1 Background

You can read and think about this section away from the computer.

5.1.1 What you are going to do

One of the most successful ways to learn to use a computer is to explore. This chapter helps you to explore a word processor program to work with tables of information.

5.1.2 What a table is

A table consists of information arranged in **columns** and **rows** of **cells,** as in the three examples below.

Notice that a table:

Each separate space on the table is called a cell.

- **may include text and numbers**
- **may have borders (lines between rows and columns) or else might not**
- **may just look like typed text (as in Table 2, below).**

Table 1

In these examples, the information in each cell only takes up one line. You will find it easiest to start with a table like this.

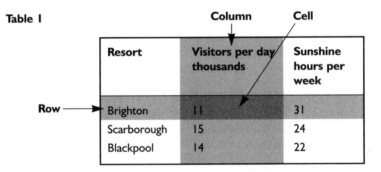

Resort	Visitors per day thousands	Sunshine hours per week
Brighton	11	31
Scarborough	15	24
Blackpool	14	22

Table 2

Reason for absence	With/without pay
Sickness	With pay
Urgent personal business	Discretionary
Interview for another job	With pay
Removal of house	Without pay

Table 3

English	French	Italian	Spanish
book	libre	libro	libro
door	porte	porta	puerta
table	table	tavola	mesa

You *could* produce something like Table 2 by typing spaces or pressing the **Tab** key between the words, but it is generally better to use a table because:

- **using spaces is unlikely to make the columns line up accurately**
- **how your text looks may change significantly on different printers if you just use spaces**
- **using a table makes it easier to change the layout of the table**
- **a table can have borders (lines between the rows and columns)**
- **using a table is easier and more flexible than using tabs.**

Whenever you need to lay information out in columns, you should consider using a table. In most cases, it is likely that you will produce a table as part of a larger piece of writing, eg a report or assignment.

5.1.3 Identify a suitable task

Many learners find it more effective to learn by carrying out a real task at the computer. You will practise all of the skills you need, and may remember what you have learnt more effectively.

It's best to choose something which is not urgent – things do go wrong while you are learning to use IT, and you should treat this as a chance to learn, more than as a chance to produce an essential piece of work. Practising on a task which is complex, large, or urgent, may put pressure on you which could prevent you from learning most thoroughly.

You may wish to pick a task which is linked to a subject that you are studying. However, if you cannot at this stage think of a suitable task, you could try copying one or more of the example tables shown on page 66.

It may be a good idea to make a sketch of what you want to produce. Your sketch should include things like:

- *what will go in each of the rows and columns*
- *how you want the table to look (eg where you want **bold** text or lines).*

In this way, you will not have to design the layout of your work at the computer at the same time as you are learning to produce a table on the computer.

Make notes about /a sketch of your task here :

5.1.4 If things go wrong

Before you start – reflect on what you might do when things go wrong. If you worked through the previous chapters, you will have identified useful strategies such as:

People use 'word processor' to mean either *a machine like a typewriter which does only word-processing,* or *a general purpose computer (a PC) running a word-processor program. Either type may be able to make tables.*

- **trying the Undo facility**
- **asking for help, either from someone nearby or a Help Desk / advisory service**
- **reading the manual**
- **using the Help facility**
- **exploring**
- **making notes on what went wrong, what you did, and what happened**
- **if all else fails, Exit from the program you are using and start again.**

5.2 Producing a table

You will find it best to work through this section at the computer. You may find it useful to make notes as you work through.

The process of putting information into a table varies with different computers and word processors, and for any given program there may be a number of different ways of doing it. The approach used in this chapter is to:

- **tell the word processor that you want to produce a table, specifying how many columns you want**
- **put the information you want into the table**
- **adjust the appearance of the table as necessary.**

5.2.1 Telling the word processor to produce a table

You need to tell the word processor you wish to produce a table. You could find out how to do this by:

- **exploring the menus – look for an item like Insert Table**
- **exploring the toolbars – for something that looks like a table**
- **using the Help facility – try looking up 'Table'**
- **looking in a booklet or manual for your particular word processor**
- **asking someone.**

Make a note here of how you tell your word processor that you wish to produce a table.

You will often need to tell the word processor how many columns and rows you require in your table. Two common ways of doing this are:

- **filling in a dialog box like this:**

It is sometimes easier to start your table with only one row. Most word-processors have an easy way of adding extra rows automatically to the end of a table (also see page 71)

NOTES

If you are unsure about how to drag see p 28.

• **in a toolbar, click on the button of a table, and drag to show how many rows and columns you want.**

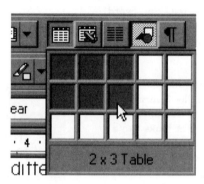

Once you have done this, you should see a representation of the table on the page in your word processor. There will probably be something (eg dotted lines) showing the rows and columns of the table.

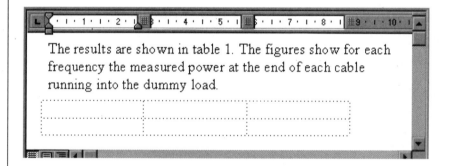

There may also be a way of drawing a table directly on the page, but to start with it will probably be simpler to use one of the methods above.

5.2.2 Putting information into the table

You can type text and numbers into the table.

Move the insertion point (the point where new text will appear on the screen) to the first cell where you want to type information. This is probably the top left cell.

To move the insertion point, use the mouse to move the cursor to where you want the insertion point, and then click.

 Start typing the contents of the first cell. When you want to type text into the second cell, you can either:

• **use the mouse again to move the insertion point to the second cell, or**
• **use a special key to move the insertion point directly to the next cell – the Tab key is the most common key, but your word processor may use a different one.**

Inside a table you may find that the **Tab** key is used to move between the cells of a table, not to leave spaces in the text as is possible outside a table.

You can continue moving between cells and typing information into your table.

In many word processors, using the special key (**Tab** or whatever your word processor uses instead) in the last (bottom right) cell of the table adds an extra row at the bottom of the table. Does this happen in your word processor?

You can use **Undo** to reverse this effect.

5.3 Altering the appearance of your table

You will find it most useful to work through this section at a computer. You may find it useful to make notes as you work through.

Now that your table contains the information you require, you may wish to change its appearance, or **format.** This section covers how to:

• **make the contents of a cell bold**
• **put lines between rows or columns (or both).**

You will also learn one way to change the width of your columns to fit the contents of the cells in each column.

5.3.1 Individual cells – changing the format

The procedure for formatting individual cells, eg to make the contents **bold,** is the same as elsewhere in a word processed document (see Chapter 4 – **Writing**). You must

• **select what you wish to change**
• **instruct the word processor to change it.**

If you wish to make the contents of a particular cell appear in **bold** text, use the mouse to select the text in that cell, and then tell the word processor you want the text in **bold.**

English	French	Italian	**Spanish**
book	libre	libro	libro
door	porte	porta	puerta
table	table	tavola	mesa

 Try this for a cell in your own table.

5.3.2 Selecting entire rows and columns

In order to change the format of a table (eg make rows of text bold, or put lines between rows or columns) you must know how to select part of the table, or in some cases the whole table. Word processors generally have some way of selecting:

- **individual cells**
- **whole rows**
- **whole columns**
- **the whole table.**

You need to find out how to do this for your word processor. The following is an example from the Help facility of one word processor:

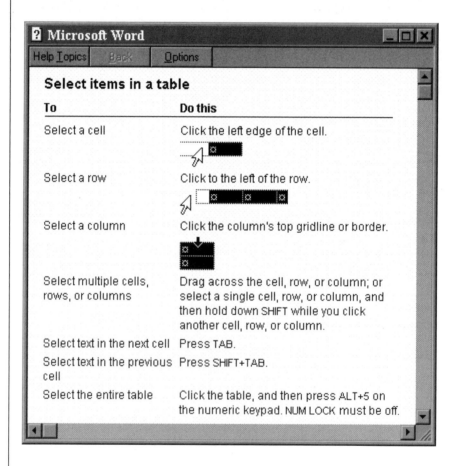

If you are unsure about how to drag see p 28.

There may also be menu entries to enable you to do these things. Try a menu labelled **Table**, or **Edit**.

It may help to make a note here of how, for your word processor, you :

- **select a cell**

- **select a row**

- **select a column**

- **select the entire table**

5.3.3 Putting lines in and around your table and using shading

Borders

You can put lines, or borders:

- **around a selected block of cells**

- **between the cells of a selected block**

- **above, below, left or right of a selected block of cells.**

Select a block of cells (or the entire table) where you want to have borders. Find out how to apply borders to the selected cells. If you wish to do this by exploring the menus or toolbars, look for:

- **menu items including the word** *Border*

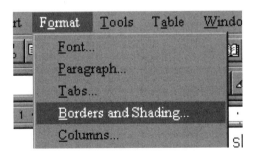

- **toolbar items which look like borders on a table**

Shading

Look at the first example table on page 66. Some of the cells have been shaded. The same principles apply to shading as to borders. Select the cells you want to change, then find a suitable menu item or button to make the change you want.

Clear	10 % shading	30% shading	50% shading

Note here the way you applied borders and shading to the selected cells in your table. Also note any mistakes you made and what you could learn from them.

5.3.4 Changing the width of columns

The widths of the columns in your table may not suit the contents of the table – there may be too much space or too little, and the table might look something like this:

Your word processor will have a way of allowing you to adjust the width of the columns to fit the text in the cells of each column. There are two main approaches – automatic and manual.

Automatic is easier, but may not be available on all word-processors. You will often find it easiest to start with automatic width and then modify the result manually to get the result you require.

Resort	Visitors	Sunsh ine
Brighton	11	31
Scarboro ugh	15	24
Blackpool l	14	22

Automatic column width

 Select the columns you wish to adjust. This will probably be the whole table, unless you have a special reason for treating some columns differently.

Find the menu item that allows you to fit the column width to the text automatically (Autofit). You could try looking at items on a **Table** menu, or a **Format** menu, or looking for anything like **Column width** or **Autofit.** If you cannot find what you want, then look in the Help system for more information.

Resort	Visitors	Sunshine
Brighton	11	31
Scarborough	15	24
Blackpool	14	22

There may not be a single menu item to 'Autofit' the column width. You may for example need to use a **Column width** *menu item to get a dialog box which contains a button to* **Autofit** *the width.*

When you adjust the column width, you may find that the lines of your table disappear off the edge of your screen. If this happens, look for arrows on the scrollbar at the bottom of the screen. Clicking or dragging the arrows will change your view of the table on the screen. Try clicking or dragging to see what happens.

 Don't forget that you can use the **undo** facility!

NOTES

Manual column width

You can also adjust the width of columns in the table manually:

- **select the columns you wish to adjust**
- **adjust the width of the selected columns.**

There are three main ways of adjusting column width manually:

- **with a dialog box like this**

Notice the **Autofit** *button in this dialog box.*

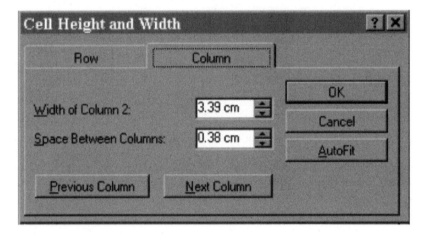

- **by dragging the column edges directly**

The cursor may change at the edge of a column to show that you can 'drag' the edge of the column to change the width

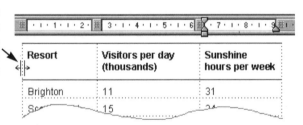

• **by dragging column markers on a 'ruler' at the top of the document window.**

Resort	Visitors per day (thousands)	Sunshine hours per week
Brighton	11	31
So~	15	2~

> Make a note here of any useful details of the method you used to change the column width.

5.4 Saving and printing your work

5.4.1 Saving your work

Every time you have made a significant number of changes in your work, you should save the new version onto disk. How often you do this will depend on how fast you work and how difficult it would be to redo everything since the last time you saved your work.

If you are not sure how to save your work, you should refer to Chapter 3 – **Beginning to Use a Computer.**

5.4.2 Printing your work

You print your table out in the same way as any other word processed document (see Chapter 4 – **Writing**).

The table may not appear *exactly* on the printed version as it did on the screen. In particular:

• **the printed version may only have those borders you added yourself, even though you might see some other borders on the screen.**
• **different printers may affect the way the table looks. Do any 'test' printing on the same printer you will use for the final version.**

• shading may particularly be affected by using different printers – experiment to find what looks best on paper, and if you are going to photocopy the final document, make sure that the photocopies also look good.

If your word-processor has a **Print Preview** facility, this will give you a better idea of what your printed work will look like.

5.5 Reflecting on your progress

You can complete this section once you have finished at the computer. It may help to look back over your notes to the previous section as you go through this section.

✔ Review here what you have learnt to do so far.
Create a table
Type text into a table
Move around in a table
Make text bold in a table
Apply borders to cells
Apply shading to cells
Resize the columns of a table

Do you feel you have succeeded in what you tried to learn? If so, what aspects of the way you worked contributed most to the success?

What, in particular, did you find difficult ?

If you have found some things difficult, you could:

- **try talking with someone who is at about the same level as you but who is not finding those particular things difficult**
- **talk to an 'expert'**
- **ask a support service**

or you may simply find it useful to take a break and come back later and have another go.

The things you have learnt with the help of this chapter are just the beginning. An introductory chapter like this cannot show just how useful the table facility of a modern word processor can be – word processors can do much more than this, and it is worth finding out more. Manuals and books specific to your own word processor may help.

6 WORKING WITH NUMBERS

6.1 Background
6.2 Putting information into the spreadsheet
6.3 Saving and printing your work
6.4 Calculating results
6.5 Changing the appearance of your spreadsheet
6.6 Reflecting on your progress

This chapter is a basic introduction to work with numbers on a computer.

It aims to help you start using numbers on a computer. It focuses on using a spreadsheet, but may be helpful in using other programs, eg some word processors allow you to do simple calculations on numbers in tables.

Before you start:

- you should already know how to start an application such as a spreadsheet
- you should understand the basic features of your computer, eg how to use windows and a mouse. Chapter 3 – *Beginning to Use a Computer* may help.

When you have completed this chapter, you will be able to:

- identify when a computer would help in working with numbers
- insert data into a spreadsheet and correct this data if necessary
- save and print a spreadsheet
- calculate results
- format a spreadsheet to change the text style
- monitor your own progress, identify successes and where you need to improve.

What you learn in this chapter will provide the basis for using and learning about any spreadsheet, on any personal computer using a graphical display (for example, running Windows).

6.1 Background

You can read and think about this section away from the computer.

6.1.1 What you are going to do

One of the most successful ways to learn to use a computer is to explore. This chapter helps you to *explore* a spreadsheet program to work with numbers.

 *Remember what you have learnt about **learning** to use a computer – you are trying to **understand** rather than to simply **know.***

When should you use a spreadsheet ?

There is no simple rule about this, but the table below should help you to decide. Use it to identify which tasks you need to do and which method might be most helpful.

There are many times when it makes most sense to use a calculator, or even pencil and paper, rather than a computer program.

Activity	Where you might use it	Suited to
Adding up columns of numbers		• Spreadsheet • Word processor • Calculator
Working with equations		• Spreadsheet • Specialist program
Drawing graphs or charts from data		• Spreadsheet • Graphing program
Doing 'what if?' calculations		• Spreadsheet • Modelling program
Making rough sketches of graphs		• Drawing program
Laying out information in a table, without any calculations		• Word processor • Spreadsheet

NOTES

6.1.2 Identify a suitable task

You will find it more effective to learn if you use this chapter in relation to a real task. You will practise the skills you need, and remember what you have learnt more effectively.

It is best to choose something which is not urgent – things do go wrong while you are learning to use IT. Treat this as a chance to learn, rather than to produce an essential piece of work. Practising on a task which is complex, large, or urgent may put pressure on you which could prevent you from learning most thoroughly.

A suitable task for this chapter is likely to involve entering a set of numbers and using groups of those numbers to produce a result.

Examples might include:

* **an invoice, showing items, prices and totals**
* **a timesheet showing the time spent on a project**
* **a set of laboratory results with a simple calculation**
* **something similar from your own areas of interest.**

The finished article is likely to look like the picture below. If you cannot think of a suitable task, you could try copying this example.

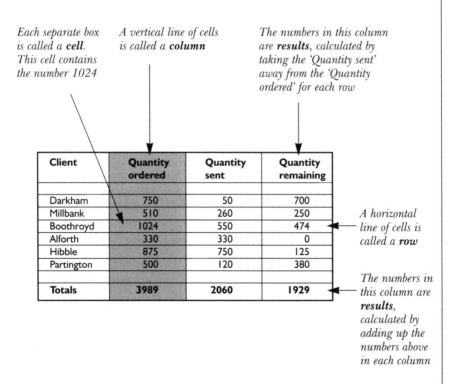

*Each separate box is called a **cell**. This cell contains the number 1024*

*A vertical line of cells is called a **column***

*The numbers in this column are **results**, calculated by taking the 'Quantity sent' away from the 'Quantity ordered' for each row*

Client	Quantity ordered	Quantity sent	Quantity remaining
Darkham	750	50	700
Millbank	510	260	250
Boothroyd	1024	550	474
Alforth	330	330	0
Hibble	875	750	125
Partington	500	120	380
Totals	**3989**	**2060**	**1929**

*A horizontal line of cells is called a **row***

*The numbers in this column are **results**, calculated by adding up the numbers above in each column*

NOTES

 It may help to plan what you want by drawing a sketch. This should include things like:

- *titles, usually at the top of columns*
- *what will go in each of the rows and columns*
- *how any results will be worked out*
- *how you want the spreadsheet to look (eg, where you want **bold** text)*

If you plan first, you will not have to practise the difficult skill of designing the layout of your work at the computer at the same time as you are learning to use the spreadsheet.

Make notes or a sketch here about your task :

6.1.3 If things go wrong

Before you start – think about what you might do when things go wrong. Chapter 3 – **Beginning to Use a Computer** identifies useful strategies such as:

- trying the **Undo** facility
- asking for help, either from someone nearby or an expert
- reading the manual
- using the **Help** facility
- exploring
- making notes on what went wrong, what you did, and what happened
- if all else fails, **Exit** from the program you are using and start again.

6.2 Putting information into the spreadsheet

You will find it most useful to work through this section at the computer and to make notes as you work through.

6.2.1 Learning to put data into the spreadsheet

Start the spreadsheet program. You should see a lot of empty boxes, or cells. These **cells** are where you will input your data. It may look something like this:

'Data' simply means information

The numbers you type might not appear in the cell until you press the Enter key.

X Microsoft Excel – Spreadsheet example

	A	B	C	D
1				
2				
3				
4				

The annotated keyboard diagram on p 63 describes some of the special typing and editing keys.

Practise putting information into each of the cells of your spreadsheet. At this stage we suggest that you concentrate on learning how to put data into the spreadsheet.

To start with, type a number (eg 235.1) and then press the **Enter** key. You should see the number appear in one of the cells, like this:

	A	B
1	235.1	
2		
3		

The cell into which your next piece of data is going will now be 'highlighted' (marked) in some way. This may be with a heavier line as shown above, or in a different colour, or in some other way.

As well as numbers, you can type text (eg headings or names of items) into spreadsheet cells. There are two main ways of doing this. Try both to see which works in your spreadsheet.

- in some spreadsheets, you simply type text and the program puts this in the highlighted cell
- in others, you must type a double quote mark (") before and after your text – the quote marks do not appear in the spreadsheet.

 Try typing some text into one of the cells. You may notice a difference in the way the text lines up in the cell – in many spreadsheets the text automatically lines up on the left and numbers on the right.

	A	B
1	235.1	
2	text	
3		

You can change which cell the next piece of data goes into by clicking with the mouse on another cell or by pressing the cursor keys to move the highlight marker around.

If you want to put something into a different cell (for example, the one in column B row 2 in the picture above) then use the mouse or the cursor keys to move the highlight to that cell before you type.

	A	B
1	235.1	
2	text	more te)
3		

Once you have typed something into B2 and pressed the **Enter** key, the highlight moves to the next cell that the spreadsheet will use – in this case, B3.

6.2.2　Exploring further

Here are two things you can try to help you explore further features of the spreadsheet.

A good way of learning the principles of IT is to try to predict what something will do before you try it out, and then see if you were right.

What do you think the **Page Up (PgUp)** key and the **Page Down (PgDn)** key will do? Make a prediction for each key and then try them out.

What you think will happen	What actually does happen

Now do the same for the **Home** and **End** keys.

What you think will happen	What actually does happen

NOTES

As you explore, some of the things that happen may surprise you.

Look at the numbers and letters at the top and left of each row and column to see where you are in the spreadsheet – the top left hand cell is usually column A row 1.

6.2.3 Correcting your work

As you type, you may make mistakes which you need to correct. The most basic way of correcting a mistake in a particular cell is to delete it.

• **Highlight the cell you want to clear using the cursor keys or mouse.**

Now you can tell the spreadsheet to clear the cell:

• **look for a Delete key on the keyboard**
• **look for a Clear button – for example**
• **find a Clear or Delete item on the menu system (often under an Edit menu).**

In this picture, the menu shows both **Clear** *and* **Delete.** *These may work in distinct ways, and you should experiment to find out which one empties the highlighted cell.*

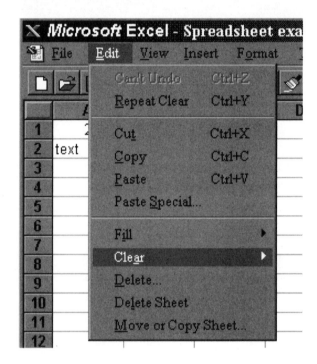

Try clearing the contents of one or more of your cells to see how this works.

You can now type in the correct text or number.

✓ Review here what you have learnt to do so far.
Type numbers into a cell
Type text into a cell
Move the highlight using the cursor keys
Move the highlight using the **PgUp, PgDn, Home** and **End** keys
Clear the contents of a cell

These are things that all spreadsheets can do. They may work slightly differently in each different spreadsheet, but the principles are the same.

6.2.4 Putting real information into your spreadsheet

Now that you've practised putting text and numbers into the cells of your spreadsheet, you can put in some real data.

 Clear all the cells so that you have an empty spreadsheet again. The most basic way of doing this is to clear each individual cell containing text or numbers, but you will probably be able to select a lot of cells by dragging the mouse to be cleared at once.

Look at the sketch you produced on page 84. This should show headings, data, where the results are going to go, and how to calculate the results (see the example on page 83).

 Using the sketch, type in the text and numbers, leaving spaces for the results that you want the spreadsheet to work out. For the example spreadsheet shown on page 83, the spreadsheet entries will look like this:

These rows have been left empty to make the table easier to read

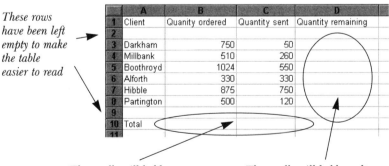

	A	B	C	D
1	Client	Quanity ordered	Quantity sent	Quantity remaining
2				
3	Darkham	750	50	
4	Millbank	510	260	
5	Boothroyd	1024	550	
6	Alforth	330	330	
7	Hibble	875	750	
8	Partington	500	120	
9				
10	Total			
11				

These cells will hold results, calculated by adding up the numbers above in each column

These cells will hold results, calculated by taking the 'Quantity sent' away from the 'Quantity ordered' for each row

NOTES

Make a note of any difficulties you have or mistakes you make that you can learn from.

Mistake or difficulty	What you have learnt from it

*If you don't know how to save or print your work, refer to Chapter 3 – **Beginning to Use a Computer** and Chapter 4 – **Writing***

6.3 Saving and printing your work

6.3.1 Saving your work

Save your work. You need a suitable name (for example *Sales* or *Project1* or *Report*). It is very important to save your work early and often.

Each time you save your work, the new version will replace the old one on your disk.

6.3.2 Printing

At points where you feel it may be useful to have a paper copy of what you have done so far, you can print your work.

Printing is usually easy. Try it and see what happens.

If you get far too much printed, or not enough, it may be because the spreadsheet contains more cells than you have used, and you **may** have to '**define the print area**' – ie tell the spreadsheet which cells you want to print. To find out how to define the print area for your spreadsheet, you could try:

* **using the Help facility**
* **looking at the options you are given when you print**
* **looking in a booklet or a manual**
* **asking someone.**

Make a note here of how you define the print area for your spreadsheet if you need to	Make a note here of how you **print** from your spreadsheet

NOTES

6.4 Calculating results

The real power of a spreadsheet lies in the way it allows you to calculate results – eg working out percentages or adding up a column of numbers. If you subsequently change some of the original data that you typed into the spreadsheet, the spreadsheet will go back and recalculate the results with the new numbers.

6.4.1 Doing a simple calculation

To do calculations, spreadsheets allow you to enter a **formula** into a cell. The formula tells the cell to carry out a calculation on some of the data you have already entered.

For example, the formula needed in the cell where column **D** meets row **3** (called cell **D3**) below will tell the spreadsheet to calculate the result by taking the value in cell **C3** away from the value in cell **B3**. This will produce a result of 750 minus 50, which is 700.

	A	B	C	D	
1	Client	Quantity ordered	Quantity sent	Quantity remaining	
2					
3	Darkham	750	50		
4	Millbank	510	260		
5	Boothroyd	1024	550		

Select one of the cells on your spreadsheet that you have left blank to take a result.

	A	B	C	D
1	Client	Quantity ordered	Quantity sent	Quantity remaining
2				
3	Darkham	750	50	
4	Millbank	510	260	
5	Boothroyd	1024	550	

Tell the spreadsheet that you are going to put a formula into the cell. You need to find out how to do it for your spreadsheet. Try:

- **typing an equals sign (=). This is the way for many spreadsheets**
- **looking up the word 'formula' in the Help facility.**

Now give the spreadsheet the formula (the calculation we want it to do) for the highlighted cell. In the example shown above, the calculation is to take the value in cell **C3** away from the value in cell **B3,** ie we want it to calculate **B3 - C3.**

You can try doing this in two different ways:

- click on the cell **B3**, then type a minus (-) symbol, then click on the cell *C3.* Each time you click or type, you should see a change on the screen
- type **B3 - C3**. This will work for many spreadsheets, but you may have to type something more complex – looking up the word *Formula* in the Help facility will help.

Note – the formula may not be visible in the cell; you may see it instead appearing somewhere near the top of the screen.

D3		=B3-C3		
	A	B	C	D
1	Client	Quantity ordered	Quantity sent	Quantity remaining
2				
3	Darkham	750	50	=B3-C3
4	Millbank	510	260	
5	Boothroyd	1024	550	

Once you have entered the formula, press the **Enter** key to complete the calculation. You should see a number (the result of the calculation) in the cell where you typed the formula, like this:

NOTES

	A	B	C	D
1	Client	Quantity ordered	Quantity sent	Quantity remaining
2				
3	Darkham	750	50	700
4	Millbank	510	260	
5	Boothroyd	1024	550	

The spreadsheet now calculates the result and puts it into the cell. The highlight is now ready on the next cell.

Once you have successfully put a formula into a cell, make a note here of how you did it.

The spreadsheet knows whether a cell contains a number that you have typed in (called a **Value***) or a* **Formula** *which produces a number as a result of a calculation.*

 Try putting formulae in other cells in the spreadsheet.

There are other **operators** that you can use in a similar way to the minus sign. You can do a lot with the 'basic four', ie:

+   plus

-      minus

*   multiply

/   divide

Notice that the multiply and divide symbols are not the same ones as those used in ordinary written maths

NOTES

In most cases, the spreadsheet will do this calculation automatically. However, in some cases you may need to find a way to tell it to **Recalculate** *or* **Calculate Now.**

6.4.2 Changing values

In the example on page 83, the spreadsheet used the values 750 and 50 from cells **B3** and **C3** to work out what should be in cell **D3.** If you change the value in cells **B3** or **C3** (eg because you have new information), then the spreadsheet will recalculate the value that appears in cell **D3.**

 Try changing one of the numbers that the spreadsheet is using in its calculation. In the example, you could change the value in cell **B3** or **C3** (or both, if you wish). Press the **Enter** key after each change.

What happens?

6.4.3 Adding up a column of numbers

You may need to add up a lot of numbers, eg a column of numbers like the ones shown here.

	A	B	
1	Client	Quanity ordered	Qu
2			
3	Darkham	750	
4	Millbank	510	
5	Boothroyd	1024	
6	Alforth	330	
7	Hibble	875	
8	Partington	500	
9			
10	Total		
11			

You *could* use a longer version of the formula method you have already seen – for example, giving the cell **B10** the formula

B3 + B4 + B5 + B6 + B7 + B8

and this would work, but for adding up lots of numbers this is not very efficient.

There is another type of formula which will work on a **range** of cells. The actual details of the formula you type, and how you tell the spreadsheet which cells to add up, will depend on the spreadsheet you are using.

For example, a common method to add up a block of cells is:

- **type the equals sign (or whatever tells the spreadsheet you want to type a formula)**
- **type a keyword such as Sum, which indicates what you want to do with the contents of the cells**
- **type a left bracket (**
- **highlight the block of cells by dragging – this *should* put something which defines the range of cells into the formula**
- **type a right bracket)**
- **press the Enter key.**

The formula may look something like the following picture:

B10	▼	=SUM(B3:B7)	
	A	**B**	**C**	
1	Client	Quantity ordered	Quantity sent	Qua
2				
3	Darkham	750	100	
4	Millbank	510	260	
5	Boothroyd	1024	550	
6	Alforth	330	330	
7	Hibble	875	750	
8	Partington	500	120	
9				
10	Total	3489		
11				

*The block of cells is written in this spreadsheet as **B3:B7**, called a **range**. Your spreadsheet may have a slightly different way of showing a range*

The values in these cells will be added together

The total will go in this cell

Make a note here of how you enter this type of formula in your spreadsheet.

Once you have successfully entered a formula like this for one cell, you can complete the other 'results' cells in your spreadsheet

✔ Review here what you have learnt to do so far.
Save your work
Define a print area
Print your work
Enter a simple formula
Change a value that the spreadsheet is using to work out a result
Add up a block of numbers

6.5 Changing the appearance of your spreadsheet

You may want to change the way some of the text or numbers appear on the printout of your spreadsheet, eg you may wish to have headings in **bold** or make certain cells appear in *italic*.

It is a good idea to plan the general appearance of your document in advance.

The general approach to changing the appearance of a cell (called **formatting** it) is as follows.

1. Highlight the cell or cells you wish to change. You can do this by clicking on a single cell or by **dragging** the mouse to select a group of cells.

2. Tell the computer how you want to change the highlighted cells, eg if you want to change it to **bold**. There may be a number of different ways of doing something on a computer, even within a single program, and you may need to:

- click on a **Bold** button on a toolbar
- choose something from a menu which allows you to change text to bold
- or you may find other ways of doing it which suit the way you like to work.

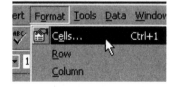

If you haven't already experimented with changing cells to **bold**, or *italic*, then you could try now, eg changing headings to **bold**, and selecting a couple of results to change to *italic*.

Once you have made all your changes for this session at the computer, save your work, and print it if you want.

Exit from the program, and close down the computer properly. You should already know how to do this, but if not you should refer to the Chapter 3 – **Beginning to Use a Computer.**

6.6 Reflecting on your progress

You can complete this section once you have finished at the computer. It may help to look back over your notes.

✔ Review here what you have learnt to do so far.
Identify when a computer would help in working with numbers
Insert data into a spreadsheet and correct this data if necessary
Save and print a spreadsheet
Calculate results
Format spreadsheet cells

NOTES

Remember – using **Undo** *or pressing the* **Escape** *key may get you out of trouble.*

Do you feel you have succeeded in what you tried to learn? If so, what aspects of the way you worked contributed most to the success?

What, in particular, did you find difficult?

If you have identified some aspects of working with numbers on a computer which you find difficult, you could:

- **try talking with someone else who is at about the same level as you but who is not finding those particular things difficult**
- **talk to an 'expert'**
- **ask at a helpdesk or support service**

or you may simply find it useful to take a break and come back another time to have another go.

What you have learnt with the help of this chapter is just a start. An introductory chapter like this cannot show just how useful a spreadsheet can be.

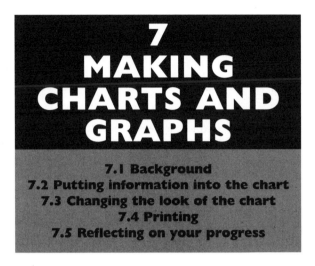

7
MAKING CHARTS AND GRAPHS

7.1 Background
7.2 Putting information into the chart
7.3 Changing the look of the chart
7.4 Printing
7.5 Reflecting on your progress

This chapter is a basic introduction to making charts on a computer.

It aims to help you produce charts and graphs based on tables of numbers. The examples and pictures illustrate the general principles common to producing charts on personal computers.

Before you start:

- you should already know how to start a suitable application such as a word processor or spreadsheet
- you should understand the basic features of your computer, eg how to work with windows and a mouse. You may find that Chapter 3 – *Beginning to Use a Computer* helps you to get to this point
- It may help to have worked through Chapter 5 – *Making Tables,* and Chapter 6 – *Working with Numbers.*

When you have completed this chapter, you will be able to:

- identify an appropriate program to produce the chart or graph required
- instruct the program to make a chart or graph
- enter data and titles to define your chart or graph
- change the appearance of the chart or graph if necessary
- print the chart or graph to an appropriate standard of presentation
- monitor your own progress, identify successes and where you need to improve.

What you learn in this chapter will provide the basis for producing graphs and charts, using any appropriate program (including word processors, presentation graphics programs and spreadsheets) on any personal computer using a graphical display (for example, running Windows).

7.1 Background

You can read and think about this section away from the computer.

7.1.1 What you are going to do

One of the most successful ways to learn to use a computer is to explore. In this chapter, we help you to explore a chart-making tool.

> *Remember to keep in mind the strategies you have already learnt to assist you as you learn a new computer program or task.*

7.1.2 Identify a suitable task

Many students find it more effective to learn by carrying out a real task at the computer. This way you are likely to remember more effectively what you have learnt. However, practising on a task which is complex, is large, or must be finished urgently, is likely to put pressure on you which could prevent you from learning most thoroughly. You need to identify a suitable task that will allow you to practise and learn without the risk of taking on something too difficult or losing lots of important work.

A suitable task is likely to involve producing a chart similar to one of these :

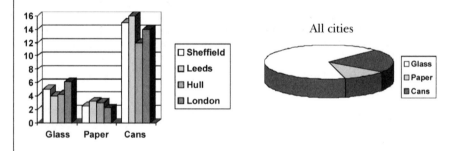

Barchart   Pie chart

See page 104 for other example charts and graphs.

See page 104 for other example charts and graphs.

> *It may be a good idea to have the data for the chart you want to produce handy and perhaps make a sketch of what you want it to look like.*

So – identify a suitable task. Treat this as a chance to learn rather than a chance to produce an essential piece of work.

Make notes or a sketch here about your task. Say what kind of chart or graph you want. Look at the examples on pages 100 and 104 for suggestions.

7.1.3 Decide which program to use

A number of different programs could be used to produce charts and graphs. Typically these might include:

- **spreadsheets**
- **word-processors**
- **presentation graphics packages**
- **desk-top publishing (DTP) programs**
- **specialist programs which** *only* **make charts and graphs.**

Often there is a trade-off between ease of use and power. That is, the easier a program is to use, the less sophisticated are the charts and graphs it can produce and the fewer choices of how your chart will appear. A spreadsheet, for example, may have very flexible and powerful tools for making charts, but may be more difficult to use than some other programs.

NOTES

All the programs suggested may be able to produce charts and graphs, in addition to their main functions.

7.1.4 General concepts

Usually, the way to make a chart or a graph involves:
1. indicating that you wish to make a chart – *Starting a chart*, p102
2. making or editing a table containing the numbers and labels for the chart – *Editing the data*, p103
3. altering the way that the chart itself looks – *Changing the look of the chart*, p103

Step 2 may come before step 1 in some programs. Explore or look in the manual or Help for your program.

7.2 Putting information into the chart

It is important to work through this section at the computer. Have a pen ready – you may find it useful to make notes as you work through.

 Start your program with a new piece of work. If you are not sure how to do this, you could try:

- **exploring**
- **looking at Chapter 3 – *Beginning to Use a Computer***
- **looking at booklets or manuals for your program**
- **asking for help.**

What happens next depends on the kind of program you're using. Some will have a table on the screen for you to put your data into. Others need to be told first that you want to make a chart.

 If your screen already shows the gridlines for a table skip this next step and go to Section 7.2.2.

7.2.1 Starting a chart

You may get the chance at this stage to say which kind of chart you want.

Look for some way to indicate that you want to make a chart. This could be in one of the menus (often the **Edit** or **Insert** menu), or there could be a button with a picture of a chart on it.

Once you've succeeded in getting a table on the screen, you're ready to put your numbers and titles in.

7.2.2 Editing the data

The computer starts your chart by asking you to make a table with the information it needs to produce the chart. Chapter 6 – **Working with Numbers,** gives you more information about using tables of numbers, but in this chapter we give you a short summary to remind you how to approach this.

In most cases you will need to type your titles and numbers into a table like this one, or change the titles and numbers in an example table which is made automatically when you indicate that you want to make a chart.

All you will need to do is :

1. Point to one of the boxes (cells) in the table with your mouse and click.

	A	B	C	D
1	Recycling	Glass	Cans	Paper
2	Sheffield	5	2.5	15
3	Leeds	4	3.2	16
4	Hull	4.3	3	12
5	London	6.1	2.2	14
6				

A row is a line of cells across the page; a column runs up and down the page.

2. Type your word or number. (If there's something in the cell already, your number or word will replace it.)

To select a row or column, you may need to click on the button marked 1, 2, 3… or A, B, C… for the row or column you want.

3. Press **Enter** or click elsewhere with your mouse for each cell you want to use.

If you have to delete columns or rows from an example table you will need to :

1. select the row or column
2. find a delete button or key, or find a menu (perhaps the **Edit** menu) with a **Delete** command

7.3 Changing the look of the chart

You may now be able to see both a table and a chart on your screen. If you only have a table, you may need to :

1. select the entire table
2. find a chart button or find a menu (perhaps the **Insert** menu) with a **Chart** or **Object** command
3. drag a rectangle with the mouse to show how big you want the chart.
4. answer a number of questions about how you want your chart to look. If in doubt, click on **OK** or **Next**.

NOTES

Look at your chart. If it's not just how you want it, decide what you'd like to change, for example :

- **the type of chart (pie-chart, scatter-graph...)**
- **the colours and patterns of each part of the chart**
- **axes and grid-lines**
- **titles.**

You'll be able to do this by :

- **finding an item in a menu (often the Format menu) to do what you want**
- **double-clicking on the thing you want to change**
- **finding a button, for example, like these for altering chart type, axes and colours, respectively.**

There are very many different types of chart. You will need to decide which kind will help your readers understand what you're showing them. Try a range of chart types and see which one suits your purpose.

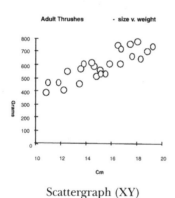

Scattergraph (XY)

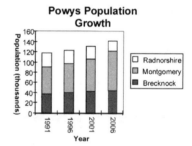

Stacked bar chart
or stacked column chart

Now save your work. (If you don't know how to save your work, refer to Chapter 3 – Beginning to Use a Computer.)

You will need to think of a suitable name (for example *Pie* or *Graph*). It is very important to save your work early and often. The next time you save your work, the new version you save will replace the old version on your disk.

7.3.1 If things go wrong

Remember to try the **Undo** facility. You should already know how to use this to undo mistakes, but it is a good idea to practice using it with this program as you use it. To help you explore, you could fill in the following information about **Undo** on your system.

> How do you undo something in the program you are using?
>
>
> When you have made a change to a chart, does using **Undo** work as you expected?

If unexpected things happen, you should first make a note of what you did just before. Then you can try:

- pressing an **Escape** key
- looking for an 'opposite' of what you just did (eg, if you pressed a key called **Page Down,** then you could try pressing **Page Up**)
- looking for an option that says **Cancel**
- repeating what you did – this may either cancel what you have done, or else may help you to understand how you made the mistake so you don't do it again
- asking someone for help – especially if what happened seems very strange to you; you could waste a lot of time trying to work something out when someone else might be able to tell you the answer quickly.

> To help you in the future, make a note of what you did to sort out a problem, what happened, and how you fixed it.

7.4 Printing

If you are given a choice of printers, you should be aware of the following :

Draft/Dot Matrix printer	Laser/BubbleJet/Inkjet Printer
• may not show how the graph will finally print out • may not even print the graph at all • usually cheap	• will usually print the chart well • you may need to edit it again to get clearer distinctions between the different parts of the chart • may cost you more money to print a high quality copy

 Try printing your work now. Printing is usually quite easy. If you don't know how to print, you should look again at Chapter 4 – **Writing.**

Remember to save your work, and print it if you want, once you have made all your changes for this session at the computer.

Finally, you should exit from your program, and close down the computer properly. You should already know how to do this, but if not, you should refer to Chapter 3 – **Beginning to Use a Computer.**

7.5 Reflecting on your progress

You can complete this section once you have finished at the computer. It may help to look back over your notes to the previous section.

✔ Review here what you have learnt to do so far.
Start a new chart
Edit the example or type in new words and numbers
Alter some aspects of how the chart appears

Do you feel you have succeeded in what you tried to do? If so, what contributed most to the success?

What did you find difficult?

If you have identified something you find difficult, you could:

- **talk with someone else at about the same level as you but who is not finding those particular things difficult**
- **talk to an expert**
- **visit a helpdesk or contact a support service**
- **take a break and come back another time and have another go.**

Are you happy with what you have produced? Could it be better? To help you to decide what you want to learn about next, look at charts and graphs in newspapers, journals or books. Explore the features of your program to see what it's capable of.

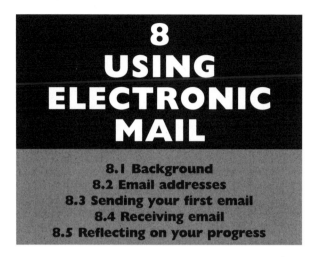

8
USING ELECTRONIC MAIL

8.1 Background
8.2 Email addresses
8.3 Sending your first email
8.4 Receiving email
8.5 Reflecting on your progress

This chapter is a basic introduction to using electronic mail (email).

It aims to help you get started in the use of email and to send and receive messages. The examples and pictures come from a range of different systems, and show the general principles of using email on personal computer systems. This chapter is particularly aimed at email systems which use the Internet, but what you learn may apply to other systems such as internal company email systems.

Before you start:

- You should understand the basic features of your computer, eg using windows and a mouse. Chapter 3 – *Beginning to Use a Computer* helps you get to this point.

When you have completed this chapter, you will be able to:

- identify how email works and in what way it might be useful to you
- find email addresses
- send, read and reply to email messages
- take appropriate action to cope with the unexpected or when things start going wrong
- identify the meaning of particular computer terms
- identify and use appropriate sources of help
- identify effective ways to learn IT skills
- identify your learning as a result of making mistakes
- monitor your own progress, identify successes and where you need to improve.

What you learn in this chapter will help you to use and learn about any electronic mail system, on any personal computer using a graphical display (for example, running Windows).

8.1 Background

You can read and think about this section away from the computer.

8.1.1 How electronic mail works

Everyone using email has a unique address to help the system find the right post-office. The diagram gives an overview of the way an electronic mail system works to get messages between you and somebody else. It is not important to remember the detail of this diagram – but it does give a picture of what is going on when you send and receive email messages.

Although the term 'post-office' is widely used in talking about electronic mail, you may also hear this referred to as a Mail Server.

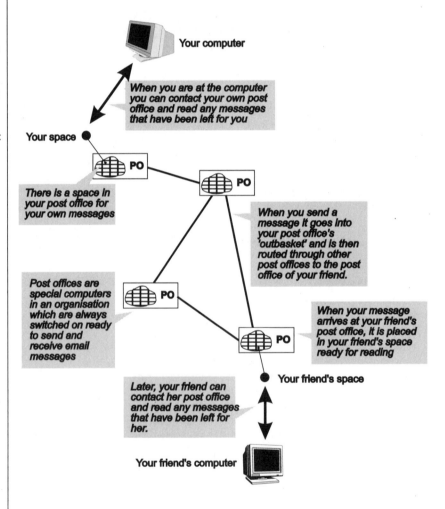

Your computer

When you are at the computer you can contact your own post office and read any messages that have been left for you

Your space

PO

PO

There is a space in your post office for your own messages

When you send a message it goes into your post office's 'outbasket' and is then routed through other post offices to the post office of your friend.

Post offices are special computers in an organisation which are always switched on ready to send and receive email messages

PO

PO

When your message arrives at your friend's post office, it is placed in your friend's space ready for reading

Your friend's space

Later, your friend can contact her post office and read any messages that have been left for her.

Your friend's computer

8.1.2 What you are going to do

One of the most successful ways to learn to use a computer is to *explore*.

Many learners find it more effective to learn by carrying out a real task at the computer. This way you are likely to practise all of the skills you need, and you may find that you remember what you have learnt more effectively than if you simply carry out a series of exercises.

This chapter will help you practise sending emails to somebody else and receiving them.

> *Remember that learning how to use a computer requires more than simply memorising which buttons to press. You need to try and develop an understanding of how the computer behaves.*

8.1.3 If things go wrong

Before you start – reflect on what you might do when things go wrong. If you have worked through Chapter 3 – **Beginning to Use a Computer** you will have identified useful strategies such as:

- **asking for help**
- **reading the manual**
- **using the Help facility**
- **exploring**
- **making notes on what went wrong, what you did, and what happened**
- **if all else fails, Exit from the program you are using and start again.**

8.1.4 Why use email?

	For	Against
email	• record of what's sent • little delay • time differences are not important • can attach documents • may be free	• the other person may not have email
post	• everyone has a postal address • can send bulky items	• may be slow • costs money
fax	• quick • record of what's sent	• other person may not have fax
phone	• immediate • can pick up on feelings	• person may not answer • can't send written material or pictures • no record of what's sent

When would email be useful for you? What other forms of communication might be better (eg phone)?	
Use for email	Alternatives to email

8.2 Email addresses

NOTES

Chapter 9 –
Surfing the World Wide Web gives you more information about Internet Service Providers.

You will need to work through this section before you start trying to send or receive email messages.

8.2.1 Your own email address

Before you can start sending and receiving email messages, you will need your own email address. Getting an email address usually means registering with an organisation which has access to the Internet (such as a university, a business, or an Internet Service Provider).

When you register for email you will be given an email address. It is important that you record this, as you will need to give it to anyone who wants to contact you via email. The actual details of your email address will depend on the organisation providing the email service, but if it uses a system that goes via the Internet, it will look something like these:

vw@alpha.hsholland.nl
v.a.woolf@geo2.poptel.org.uk
virginia@rockisland.com
woolf_virginia@emk.com
virginia.woolf@student.shu.ac.uk

If you gave this last address verbally, you would pronounce it:
virginia dot woolf at student dot s h u dot a c dot uk

The following is an explanation of what the parts of the address mean:

virginia.woolf = *a person*
student =*name of computer which handles (student) email*
shu =*Sheffield Hallam University*
ac = *academic*
uk = *United Kingdom.*

> *It is extremely important to copy your email address accurately as a small mistake will mean that the email will not get through. **Everything** in the address is important – the dots and any other special symbols like an underscore (_) as well as the letters and numbers. Note that there are **no** spaces in the email address and there is **no** dot at the end of it.*

You may find it useful to record your own email address here :

You may also be given a login code and a password to get you into the email system. You will also need to remember these, but it is **not** a good idea to keep a record of the password where it can be found by the wrong people.

The login code may be described in your system by other words, like 'login ID' or simply 'ID', 'access code' or 'username'.

Keep your password secure – if you think someone else might know your password, change it! And don't use someone else's login code and password, even for a joke.

8.2.2   Finding other people's email addresses

When someone has sent you an email, their address is often shown somewhere near the top of the message.

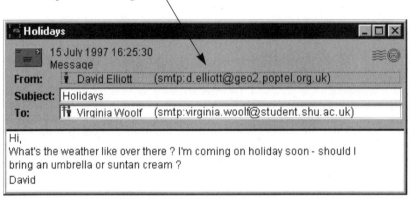

See page 119 for how to reply to an email you've received – you won't need to know the other person's address as replies are addressed automatically.

Many organisations provide a way to find people's email addresses. This may be accessible through the World Wide Web (see Chapter 9 – **Surfing the World Wide Web**) or there may be a special email directory program to use.

These services are sometimes linked together so that you can find addresses for email users at many organisations through a single service.

Some email programs provide a simple link into the directory service – find out whether yours does. Common names for such services are:

* **email directory**
* **X500 directory**
* **directory**
* **directory service**
* **address book**

so look out for the words 'directory' or 'address'.

Directories and address books may just show you a person's name (eg Virginia Woolf) but use the full address (virginia.woolf@student.shu.ac.uk) behind the scenes.

To find out someone else's email address, it may be simpler to contact them by other means initially – eg phone, letter.

Most email systems allow you to store email addresses which you use often in a personal 'address book' so you don't have to remember them. Look for this feature in your system when you've collected some addresses.

8.3 Sending your first email

8.3.1 Starting off

NOTES

Examples of email icons

We suggest that you practise by trying to send an email. You could send it to yourself, or to another student who has an address you know.

 Start the email program. If you are not sure how to do this, you could try:

- **exploring**
- **looking for an email icon**
- **working through 'Beginning to Use a Computer'**
- **looking at documentation for your system.**

Chapter 9 – **Surfing the World Wide Web** *gives you more information about Internet Service Providers.*

If you are using an email system provided by an Internet Service Provider (which usually means using a phone line to connect to the Internet) you may need to connect to the Internet before you start the email program. The documentation or manuals provided by your Internet Service Provider should tell you what you need to do to get into the email system.

 You may be asked at this stage for your login code and a password to get into the email system. These will be the ones you were given when you registered for email.

You may also have other login codes and passwords, for example to allow you to use the computer network.

You will need to find the part of the email system that allows you to send messages. You could try:

- **exploring the menus, looking for something that indicates that you can create or send messages, eg**

- **clicking a button which looks something to do with writing or sending a message, eg**
- **looking for a help system**
- **reading a booklet or manual**
- **asking for help.**

If you are successful, your computer screen should show what looks like a form for you to fill in. Its appearance will depend on the email system and the computer system you are using, but it will have some or all of the features shown in the following picture.

Somewhere to type a subject title – this tells the person receiving it what it is about

Somewhere to type the email address of the person you want to send it to

*Be careful – the **Enter** key may not always do what you intend. Use the mouse instead to put the cursor at the right place on the form.*

Space for actual message

You may find it useful to record here how you reached this point. If you clicked on a button, make a sketch of the button.

8.3.2 Writing and sending the message

NOTES

Work out what you want to say. If you start learning with a short message and you make a mistake, you won't have lost a lot of work.

Type the email address of the person you are sending the email to in the space provided for the address. Remember to type this accurately.

Type something in the space provided for the **Subject** or **Title**. This will tell the person who receives the message what it is about, so choose something meaningful.

Type your message in the space provided on the screen for the message.

Some email systems will allow you to type only part of the name, or to select a name from a list.

There may be other spaces or options you can choose on the email form on your screen. These may have an obvious meaning, in which case you could experiment, or they may be harder to work out. However, in most email systems you only need to have a message and an email address in order to send the email.

Do not *send offensive emails, or emails that contain material that belongs to other people. To do so is usually a serious offence. The emails that you send can be traced back to you.*

There should be a fairly obvious way of sending your email. There may be a button on the screen somewhere, eg on the email form you have just filled in or on a toolbar. Alternatively, you may need to find something like a **Send Message** item on one of the menus.

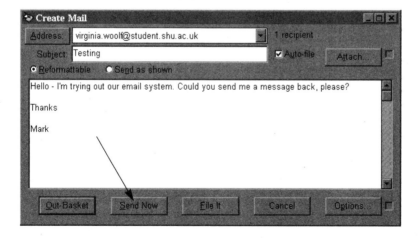

Give the message a final check before you send it. This is very important, as in most email systems you can't 'unsend' email once you've sent it. In some cases, the email system will respond to show you that the message has been sent.

> *Many (but not all) email systems keep a copy of your sent emails. If you don't want to keep them, you can delete them. You will need to find out how to do this on your system.*

Don't forget the ways you have learnt of getting out of trouble – for example pressing the **Escape** key.

Finally, if you are not going to do any more at present, you should exit from your program, and close down the computer properly. You should already know how to do this, but if not, you should refer to section 3.11 on ***Closing down your application*** in Chapter 3 – ***Beginning to Use a Computer.***

8.4 Receiving email

8.4.1 Reading your email

Email messages addressed to you will be stored in your Post Office until you start up the email program.

In most systems, to check whether you have received any email messages you simply have to start the email program and wait a little while for it to check for new messages. In others, you may have to do something to ask it to check for new messages.

Arrange for someone to send you an email. You might do this by:

Email can take from a few minutes to several hours to reach its destination. You could try sending yourself an email to see how long it takes.

- **giving someone your email address and asking them to send you an email, or**
- **sending someone an email asking them to send an email back to you.**

Allow a little time for their email to reach you, and then start up the email program again and check to see if you have any new mail.

You should see a list of the email messages waiting for you. In most cases you can look at individual messages by double clicking on them with the mouse.

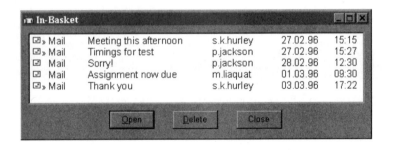

NOTES

> *Email systems generally keep a copy of the emails you have received.*
>
> *If you don't want to keep them, you can delete them. Explore and find out how to do this on your system. You may also be able to 'file' any emails you do want to keep.*

8.4.2 Replying to email

Most systems allow you to reply to received emails very easily.

Read the email you want to reply to, then look for a button or menu item marked **Reply**, or with an indication of 'return' on it. It may be :

- **on the email you have just read**
- **on a toolbar or in one of the menus, often a Message menu.**

You'll be shown a form with the address and subject already filled in – all you have to do is type in your reply.

The subject will normally say something like '**Re :**' followed by the subject of the original message, eg '**Re : Holiday**', so that the other person knows it's a reply, and which message it's a reply to.

Re *may be taken to mean 'reply' or, as in formal writing, 'in the matter of, concerning'*

The original message may be *quoted* in some way in the reply. It may appear shaded, or with each line following a > sign, or without any obvious changes in the same space where you type your reply.

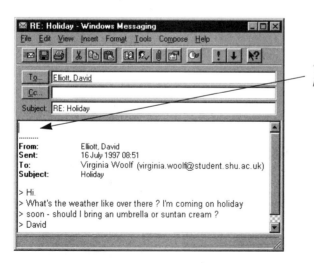

Type your reply here

 When you've typed your reply, send it in the usual way.

8.5 Reflecting on your progress

You can complete this section once you have finished at the computer. It may help to look back over your notes.

✔ Review here what you have learnt to do so far.
Your email address
Someone else's email address
How to start the email program
How to compose an email message
The value of a subject header
How to send an email message
How to receive an email message
How to reply to email messages
The need to keep your password secure

Do you feel you have succeeded in what you tried to do? If so, what aspects of the way you worked contributed most to the success?   What, in particular, did you find difficult?

If you have identified some aspects of email which you find difficult, you could:

- **try talking with someone else who is at about the same level as you but who is not finding those particular things difficult**
- **talk to an expert**
- **visit a helpdesk or consult a support service**

or you may simply find it useful to take a break and come back another time to have another go.

9
SURFING THE WORLD WIDE WEB

9.1 Background
9.2 Finding information on the World Wide Web
9.3 Making bookmarks
9.4 Improving your skills
9.5 Other things you should know about
9.6 Working more effectively
9.7 Getting an Internet connection
9.8 Reflecting on your progress

This chapter is a basic introduction to using a computer to find information on the Internet. It introduces you to the main ways of using the World Wide Web to find information, and aims to help you make the most effective use of your Internet searching.

Chapter 10 – **Retrieving Information** aims to help you improve your skills in searching for information.

This chapter does not explicitly deal with the use of email, as this is already covered in Chapter 8 – **Using Electronic Mail,** although some of what you learn in this chapter may give more foundation to your understanding of electronic mail over the Internet.

Before you start:

- **you should already know how to use basic computer applications such as a word processor**
- **you will need to have a connection to the Internet. Section 9.7 at the end of this chapter gives some information about how to get connected to the Internet.**

When you have completed this chapter, you will be able to:

- **follow links from one World Wide Web (WWW) page to another using a web browser**
- **type in an Internet address for a WWW page**
- **use a search engine to find pages**
- **save and print WWW pages**
- **save and organise bookmarks to allow you to return to useful WWW pages**
- **work efficiently in finding information on the WWW.**

The skills that you develop should be useful whatever World Wide Web browser you use, on a range of personal computers.

NOTES

The Internet is a world-wide network of linked computer networks. If your computer is connected to the Internet, you can get files from other machines on the Internet provided that (a) you know know the address of the other computer (b) you have permission to access the file on the other computer

Intranets are similar to the Internet, but are usually inside an organisation such as a company or a university. They are used to distribute internal information, and are not usually accessible from outside the organisation

9.1 Background

One of the most successful ways of learning about using computers is to explore. In this chapter, you will use a program called a **Browser** to explore the Internet, and in particular the World Wide Web, to find useful information.

9.1.1 What the Internet is

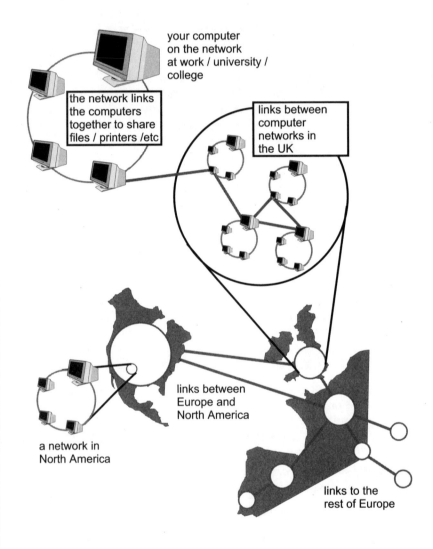

your computer on the network at work / university / college

the network links the computers together to share files / printers /etc

links between computer networks in the UK

links between Europe and North America

a network in North America

links to the rest of Europe

9.1.2 What the World Wide Web is

The World Wide Web (WWW) is a huge collection of linked pages of information on the Internet. It is so easy to use it makes the process of finding and using information accessible to anyone who has a computer with an Internet connection.

In general, you go from page to page on the World Wide Web by clicking the mouse button on particular points on a page, called links.

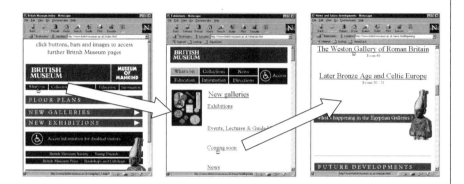

The information in the World Wide Web is not really like the information in a library:

Library	World Wide Web
Organised by subject and/or author for easy access	Not really organised at all
Has a catalogue to help you find information	Does not have a catalogue, although some 'search tools' are available
Is more or less fixed – the contents of a library do not change much from time to time	Is constantly changing – what you find tomorrow may be different from what you find today
Generally contains information which is mostly accurate	The information may or may not be accurate, and you have to exercise your own judgement.
Has one or a small number of people maintaining the collection of information	Is not maintained as a whole by anybody

Lots of people put their own information onto the World Wide Web with the intention of making it available for other people to look at and use.

NOTES

See Section 9.7 for more information about getting an Internet connection

The information on the WWW is generally organised into 'pages', each of which could contain one or more of the following:

- **text**
- **links to other pages**
- **pictures**
- **video**
- **music and sounds**
- **computer programs.**

9.1.3 Identify a suitable task

People usually find they learn best on the computer when they are practising on a real task. You will need to identify a task which will help you learn, but which, if you don't finish it or if you have problems along the way, will not be critical.

A suitable task would be to search for some information of interest to you. For example, you might search for:

- **information about a subject you are studying**
- **train or bus times**
- **a map of a particular area**
- **the words to a particular song**
- **opinions about a current political issue.**

> Make a note here of some ideas for things you might search for as you are working through this chapter.
>
>
>
>
>
>
>
>
>
>
>
>
>
>
>

Note – it may take some time to search the Internet for the information you want, especially if you are using an Internet connection from home, and a large part of this time may be spent waiting. Experienced computer users often do other work on or near the computer while they wait.

9.1.4 If things go wrong

Before you start – reflect on what you might do when things go wrong. If you worked through Chapter 3 – **Beginning to Use a Computer** and Chapter 4 – **Writing** you will have identified such strategies as:

- trying an **Undo** facility
- asking for help
- reading a manual
- using a help facility
- exploring
- making notes on what went wrong, what you did, and what happened
- if all else fails, **Exit** from the program and start again.

In addition, you might want to try the use of a **Stop** or **Back** facility (button, key, or menu item) in the program you are using.

9.2 Finding information on the World Wide Web

There are three main ways of finding information on the World Wide Web:

- starting at a known place, and following links
- typing in the address of the information you want
- using a specialised WWW page to search for what you want.

These are covered separately here, but in practice you usually use a combination of all three.

The program you are going to use is called a **browser.** The sort of name you are looking for will include words like navigate, explore, browse, and may well have the words Internet or World Wide Web somewhere in the title. The icon may include something to do with searching the world.

You may also find that other programs also have the ability to browse the World Wide Web – for example word processors or file management tools.

*If you can't find a **Home** button or menu item, and the browser doesn't start with a home page, then you should skip forward to the next section 'Type an Internet location' on page 129, and return here once you have found a WWW page to start your search from.*

9.2.1 Start at a known page and follow a link

Start up your Internet browser the way you normally start up a program. In most cases, the browser will have been set up to start with a particular page of information (called a home page), and will probably show you that page when you start the browser.

If the browser doesn't load the home page when you start, you could try looking for :

- a **Home** button
- a **menu bar item to load the home page.**

You should see a page of information. The picture below shows some of the main components that you might see on a WWW page. What you actually see may be quite different from this, but it should be built up from the same components.

Pictures

Text links to other pages — often underlined

Text

Picture links to other pages

There may be other components, and some of these will be obvious enough for you to try out as you go along. These are the main ones of interest at this point.

> Look at the WWW page on your screen, and identify some of the links. Move the mouse around so that it passes over the links without clicking the mouse button, and make a note here of what happens when you move the mouse to position the cursor over one of the links on the page.

> How are the links shown on the page you are looking at?

Click on one of the links. Wait, and watch on the screen what happens. It will take you to another page. You could also try to find a picture which contains a link (remember – the cursor will change on a link).

Try and follow a few links around to see where you can go. As you go, see if you can make a path from where you started to the information you want just by clicking on links.

At some point, it may take a while for a particular page to load from the Internet onto your computer screen. As you wait, try to answer the following questions:

How does the screen show you that something is happening as you wait? (there may be several things that you can see)

How does the text on the page appear? (all at once / in bits / etc)

How do pictures appear? (all at once / in bits / etc)

How can you tell when a page has arrived completely on your system?

Internet browsers have a way of getting back to previous screens. Search around on your system to find a button or menu item that will take you back to previous screens, and try it out.

Make a note here of the button / menu item that takes you back to the previous screens.

If a page is taking a very long time to load, you could try a number of strategies:

- **wait longer and find something else to do while you are waiting**
- **find some way to stop the loading of the page, and see if what you want appears at that point (it may!)**
- **you can generally click on links on a page as soon as you can see them – you do not have to wait for the whole page to load**
- **find a way to stop the page loading, and then try going back and reloading – it may work faster the second time (There is often a 'reload' button or menu item.)**
- **try again at a different time (see page 138 for more on this).**

9.2.2 Type an Internet location (address)

Keep a lookout for Internet addresses, which may also be called **locations,** or **URLs.** This is rather like a house address – it describes exactly where on the Internet to find a particular page of information. A URL will often begin with http:// and will look something like the one written here:

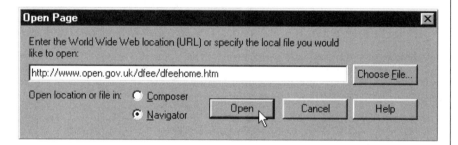

(At the time of writing, this is the URL for the Department for Education and Employment, the DfEE)

You might find URLs of interest to you:

- **on adverts**
- **in newspaper and magazine articles**
- **from friends and colleagues**
- **from tutors.**

Make a note here of at least one URL you'd like to try.

NOTES

You will have to judge for yourself if a page is loading too slowly. Try and get a feel for what is 'normal', but remember that this may change at different times of day.

It is **very** important to get URLs spelt and copied exactly, with the dots, punctuation and capital letters. Getting these wrong will probably mean the URL won't work. In particular, watch out for the difference between _ and -, and also between / and \. URLs generally have no spaces in them.

If you really can't find an URL for yourself, you could try the URL for the page that we have set up to go with this book, at

On your system, you may not need to type the http://

http://www.shu.ac.uk/services/lti/studentskills.htm

 Once you have an URL to look at, type it into the appropriate place on your browser. There may be a place visible on the screen already to type in the location, or you may have to use a menu item or a button to allow you to do this. If you need to, search the menus for something like **Open**.

New Window	Ctrl+N
Open...	Ctrl+O
Save	Ctrl+S
Save As File...	
New Message...	
Send To	▶
Page Setup...	
Print...	Ctrl+P
Create Shortcut	
Properties	
Close	

You will have to tell the computer to go and find the page at the URL you have typed in. This will usually mean either clicking on a button or pressing the **Return** key.

Having reached the page, this may be the page you want, with the information you need directly on it. If not, you may be able to click on links until you get to the specific information you want.

Did you find what you were looking for?

How long did it take you to get to the information you wanted?

Make a note here of how good the information you found is:

• **Did you find what you wanted?**
• **Is it accurate?**
• **Is it all that you wanted, or will you want to look for more?**
• **Does it contain links to other, related information?**

9.2.3   Use a search engine

One of the most effective ways to find information on the Internet is to use a specialised WWW page called a **search engine.** This is generally a page that can help you locate information if you have a word or words to start off your search.

What to look for

> Make a note here of what you are going to look for.
>
>
> Think of something fairly specific to search for (the more accurately you can define what you are looking for, the more likely you are to find something suitable reasonably quickly), and write here a few key words that will help to find what you want.

Chapter 10 – **Retrieving Information** *goes into more detail about finding good words with which to start a search.*

If you start from someone else's pages, they may offer you the choice of either searching the site or searching the Web / WWW / Rest of the World.

Where to look

You are going to use a search engine. In order to find a search engine, you can:

* **start from your home page or another page to find a search engine (If you don't have a good starting page, the page associated with this book contains links to some search engines, and most university home pages will also have links to search engines.)**
* **find a Search button or menu item on your browser**
* **keep lists of URLs for search engines.**

NOTES

Remember the
Back facility
to return you
to the previous
page

Use your Internet browser to find a search engine page. These do change quite frequently, but part of one search engine page is shown below.

Notice the link
to 'Help' on
this WWW
page.

Look for a **Help** item, or an example to show you how to type in your search.

Generally what you do is type in a word or words, and tell the Search engine to go and search (there may be a search button on the page, or you may just have to press the **Enter** key). The help for your search engine will probably tell you more.

Type one or more words to define your search into the appropriate place on the search engine page, and click a **Search** button or press **Enter**.

Typically what you will get from a search will be a page containing links. It may also tell you how many times it has found your search terms.

NOTES

Chapter 10 –
Retreiving
Information
*gives you some
guidance on
searching
effectively.*

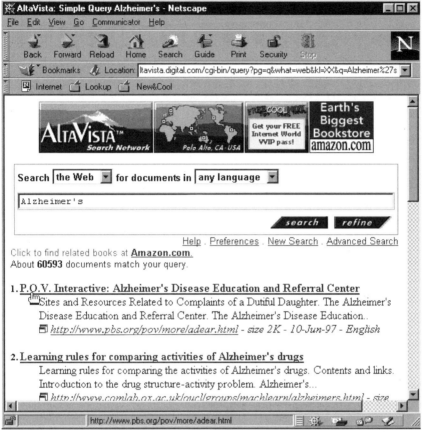

You will need to evaluate what you have found to see whether the terms you have used resulted in a useful set of links. There may, like in the example shown above, be far too many results, or the hits that the search engine has found may not be appropriate to your needs.

In general, the first links that the search engine shows are the ones closest to the words you gave it, and the last ones are most loosely related to the words you entered. You may well get a chance to look at a couple of lines of text from each page that the search engine has found.

Follow one or more of the links from the search engine's results page to see how useful they are for your search. You may find some of the pages that the search engine leads you to useful as starting points for further exploration.

9.3 Making bookmarks

Having found a useful page, it is often a good idea if you can keep a note of where to find it again. You could write down the URL, or you could use the **Copy** and **Paste** facilities on your computer to copy the URL into a word processed document, for example.

However, WWW browsers generally have a facility to keep a record of useful places. You can ask the program itself to record the location of the page (the URL) together with some sort of description of the page. The next time you want to go to that page, you can then select it from a menu.

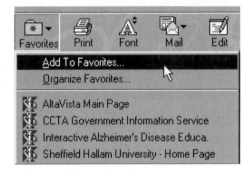

 Try it now. Find a page that you think you might want to visit again. Look on your browser for the way to record useful locations. Words you might look for include **Bookmark** and **Favourite**, and you want to **Add** a location.

Go and visit some other pages, and then use the stored location to return to the site that you recorded.

Note – the contents of WWW pages may change from time to time, so don't be surprised if a link is different the next time you look at it.

9.3.1 Organising your bookmarks

Browsers also usually allow you to organise your bookmarks, so that you can file them into some sort of folder structure, just as you can with files on a disk (see Chapter 12 – **File Management** for more advice on sensible approaches to filing).

 Explore the browser that you use to find out how to organise the structure of your bookmarks. This is likely to involve dragging individual bookmarks up and down a diagram of the bookmark filing system.

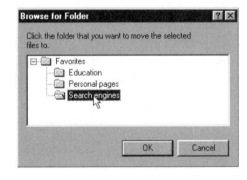

9.4 Improving your skills

One of the things that you should have learnt by now about using a computer is that it is important to explore, to try out new things, and to keep an inquisitive mind. This is particularly true of using the Internet. You may have your own favourite ways of working, but things change so frequently on the Internet that it is essential to keep looking for new approaches and ways of working.

So you should be curious. You should try out new things frequently. For example, you may find that you have your own favourite search engine, but from time to time you should try:

- **testing out other search engines that you don't normally use, to see if they have changed or improved, or if they might be more suitable for some types of searches**
- **looking for other search engines using your own search engine (try using the phrase 'search engine' in a search)**
- **asking friends what search engines they use**
- **looking on home pages – for example university home pages – to see what they are suggesting that their students and staff use**
- **getting into a spirit of exploring – this is important both for getting good results and for keeping up-to-date.**

9.5 Other things you should know about

9.5.1 Saving Web pages

Web browsers generally give you the ability to save pages from the Internet. This may be useful if you find some information (or links) that you want to be able to refer to again.

However, each web page is usually made up of several files, one or more containing the text and the structure of the page, and further files containing the pictures, or graphics, on the page. Depending on your browser, and also depending on how you ask it to save a page, you may find that it has saved:

- **the page as you found it, complete with all graphics**
- **just the text and structure, without the graphics**
- **the complete structure of the whole local web (ie the collection of pages in that particular 'set' of pages).**

Having saved a page, you can open the page with the Web browser in the same sort of way that you would open a written document in a word processor, even if your computer is not at that time connected to the Internet.

Copyright warning: Although pages on the World Wide Web may appear to be freely available to anyone who wants them, they usually have similar copyright rules to other published material, and you may need to get the permission of the authors and any other copyright holders in order to make copies or to use them for anything else.

Try saving one or more pages from the World Wide Web to your own computer disk, and then open the saved copy from disk to see how the browser has dealt with the process of saving.

Be warned that in some cases links and other items on the pages that you have saved may not work on your saved copy in the same way that they do on the original versions on the Internet.

9.5.2 Printing pages

Web browsers usually give you the ability to print the information from pages you see on screen. Because of the structure of Web pages (described above) what you produce using a printer may not be exactly what you see on screen. However, printing is a useful way of copying and recording information from the Web.

 Try printing one or more pages from your browser to see how well the pages compare with what you see on screen.

9.6 Working more effectively

Very often, the Internet is slower than you would like. There are a number of things that you can do to make your use of the Internet more effective and efficient. Chapter 10 – **Retrieving Information** may give you some ideas about effective searching, but some of the other things you can do to make the best use of your time include:

- **turing off auto-loading of images**
- **opening links in new windows**
- **choosing the best times of day to access the Internet.**

These are explained in some more detail in the following sections.

To find out how to do this in your browser, use the help system or explore the menus for anything which deals with automatic loading of images. You may need to ask someone how to do this.

9.6.1 Turning off auto-loading of images

If you are finding it takes a long time for the pages you are using to download from the Internet to your computer, you might want to consider turning off the automatic loading of images.

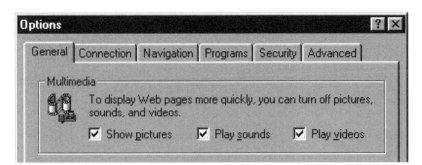

Remember that an Internet page is often made up of several different files – text, structure, pictures –– and that the pictures are often the largest of these, and hence the slowest to reach you. You can usually tell your browser not to load the images (pictures) automatically, and instead you will see a page with empty 'placeholders' for the pictures. Although this page may look odd, it will often function perfectly well either as a source of text information, or as a source of links to other pages.

If you find that a particular image is important, either because you actually want to look at the picture, or because it contains links within the picture, you can tell the browser to load (or show) that image once it has retrieved the text of the page.

This is particularly useful if you are using an Internet connection from home, where you may be paying phone and Internet connection charges for each minute you are connected to the Internet.

9.6.2   Opening links in new windows

Your browser will probably allow you to work with more than one window open on the screen. This is like having two or more copies of the browser working at the same time. You can therefore look at one page, while the other browser window is off looking for another link at the same time. Often you can have several browser windows open at the same time. Chapter 11 – **Working with Several Windows** will help you to manage the use of more than one window at once.

Look for menu items like **New Window** *or* **New Browser Window**

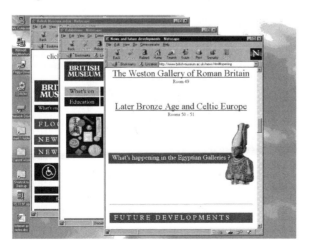

One variation of this is the ability to click on a link with a different mouse button and choose to open the link in a new window. This will leave the original page where it was, and start up a new browser window to follow the link.

9.6.3 Identifying the best times of day to access the Internet

The speed of your Internet connection, or the speed at which it can transfer to your machine information from the computer holding the page you want, will vary at different times of day. So, for example, it will often be slower trying to get Web pages to Britain from the USA during the afternoon, as people on both sides of the Atlantic are at work, and at that time enough of them may be asking for the transfer of information from the other country to mean that the speed of the link between Britain and the USA cannot keep up with the information being demanded. The result is that your information will come more slowly.

Whenever you access the Internet, use the chart below to record a tick each time when you find access particularly slow or particularly fast. This should help you to build up a picture of the best times for you to access the Internet.

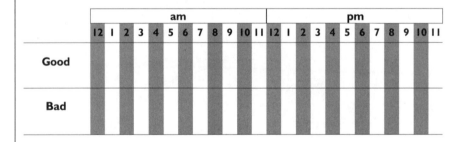

9.7 Getting an Internet connection

There are two main routes to getting Internet access:

- **You may already have access to the Internet in your place of work or study. This usually means that your Internet connection will not cost you anything. It will be taken care of by the people who manage the computer network and the other computer systems, and these will probably be the people you need to contact if you have questions about your Internet connection or the software you use.**

- **You may pay to get a connection to the Internet through a 'dial-up' connection to an Internet Service Provider (ISP). This means that, when you want to connect to the Internet, your computer dials a number on the phone line and uses the phone line as a link between you and the Internet.**

9.7.1 Getting a connection via an Internet Service Provider (ISP)

You will need the following things in order to connect to the Internet via an Internet Service Provider:

- **an account with the Internet Service Provider**
- **a phone line with standard telephone sockets**
- **a modem**
- **computer software to handle the connection at your end**
- **a browser and any other applications (eg email)**
- **a computer capable of running the software.**

You can buy a complete package, including everything except the computer, in many computer stores.

There are a number of different Internet Service Providers. Many new computers come ready with icons to allow you to sign up for an ISP automatically (provided you have a modem and phone line), but these will only deal with a few of the largest ISPs. You should be able to find information and advertisements for other ISPs from:

- **computer advisers (eg help desks or experts)**
- **computer magazines**
- **computer stores**
- **by asking someone else who already has a connection with an ISP.**

Generally, the ISP will provide you with a pack which includes the software you need to get you going, and the phone number the computer needs to dial for an Internet connection.

*A **modem** is an electronic device that goes between the computer and the phone line in order to translate between the signals that the computer understands and signals that can go down the phone line. Some computers have modems built in.*

There are three main ways in which the ISP will charge you for your Internet connection:

- **a flat rate, which allows you 'unlimited connect time'**
- **a fee which includes a number of hours' access per month; if you use more than this you get charged for any extra time, and this extra charging can be quite high**
- **a fee which includes no free access; you pay an extra amount for whatever time you use.**

In addition, you will usually have to pay your phone company the cost of the local phone charges for the time that you are connected.

9.8 Reflecting on your progress

You can complete this section once you have finished at the computer. It may help to look back over your notes to the previous sections.

✔	Tick what you have learnt to do so far.
	Identify and start a web browser
	Follow links
	Type in an internet address
	Use a search engine
	Use bookmarks to return to useful Web pages
	Improve your skills by trying out new things
	Save Web pages
	Print Web pages
	Improve the effectiveness of your work

If you have identified some aspects of learning to use the World Wide Web which you find difficult, you could:

- **talk with someone else who is at about the same level as you but who is not finding those particular things difficult**
- **talk to someone who is more expert than you**
- **contact a support service**

or you may simply find it useful to take a break and come back another time and have another go.

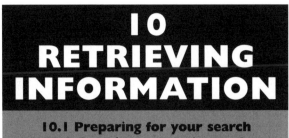

10 RETRIEVING INFORMATION

10.1 Preparing for your search
10.2 Carrying out your search
10.3 Reflecting on your progress

This chapter is an introduction to retrieving information, which could be in the form of text, numbers, charts, graphs, sounds, pictures and photographs stored on a computer for those who:

- **are beginning to retrieve information**
- **have a little experience but need a refresher**
- **would like to build up confidence.**

This chapter helps you retrieve computerised information efficiently and effectively.

Before you start:

- you should understand the basic features of your computer, eg how to work with windows and a mouse. Chapter 3 – *Beginning to Use a Computer* and Chapter 4 – *Writing* may help you get to this point.
- you should understand the basic features of gathering and using information. The chapters on *Gathering and Using Information* in *The Student Skills Guide*, by Sue Drew and Rosie Bingham, may help.
- if you wish to retrieve information from the Internet, you should understand how to access the Internet and the basics of using the Internet tools – see Chapter 9 – *Surfing the World Wide Web*.

When you have completed this chapter, you will be able to:

- identify ways in which the computer can help you carry out an information search
- identify a source to search from
- start up a computerised information resource and tell the resource what to look for
- use on-screen information eg follow on-screen instructions
- take appropriate action to cope with the unexpected or with things going wrong
- identify and use appropriate sources of help
- evaluate whether the information found meets your needs
- identify effective ways for you to learn IT skills
- identify your learning as a result of making mistakes
- monitor your own progress, identify successes and where you need to improve.

What you learn in this chapter will help you to search for information using a wide range of information sources, including CD-ROMs, databases, library catalogues, the World Wide Web, and specialist on-line information resources, on any personal computer using a graphical display (for example, running Windows).

NOTES

10.1 Preparing for your search

You can read and think about this section away from the computer.

10.1.1 What you are going to do

A successful way to learn how to find information using a computer is to explore. This chapter helps you to learn how to do this.

> Be wary of simply copying down sequences of key presses or mouse clicks for a particular computerised information resource. It is much more effective to identify the general principles behind what you are doing. A copied sequence of actions may not work as you expect the next time you use it, because the way the computer responds will also depend on other things, such as what you were doing before you carried out the actions.

10.1.2 Identifying a suitable search

People often find it more effective to learn by carrying out a **real** task at the computer. This way you are more likely to learn. However, practising on a task which is complex, large, or must be finished quickly may put pressure on you and could prevent you from learning thoroughly. Identify a search that allows you to practise and learn without the risk of your taking on something too difficult.

Examples might include retrieving:

* **the details about what is available (books, videos and other resources) on transport**
* **what B. Gunston has published on transport**
* **train travel statistics and graphs**
* **an article on the advantages/disadvantages of motor bikes**
* **a photograph showing some of the effects of air pollution on city centre buildings**
* **electronic mail messages from the Environment Agency**
* **information about the Sheffield Canal Company Ltd**
* **an explanation of acid rain.**

Identify a task and treat this as a chance to learn.

Make notes here about your task.

10.1.3 Planning your search – some key questions

Before you search on a computerised information resource, you need to be clear about what you want to achieve to avoid wasting time, energy and effort. Identify some fundamental questions whenever you are searching for information.

What am I looking for?

What is it for and what will I do with it?

When do I need it for?

Before starting your search, you may find it helps you clarify what you are looking for if you refer to the chapters on **Gathering and Using Information** in *The Student Skills Guide,* by Sue Drew and Rosie Bingham.

NOTES

10.1.4 Preparing your search

You need to consider carefully how to tell the computer what you are looking for.

For example, if you wanted to find information on 'The effects of different modes of transport', you could search for:

- **transport or travel**
- **bus, coach, rail, cycle, plane, car, motor car, automobile**
- **advantages and disadvantages, or pros and cons**
- **organisations like Friends of the Earth or Manchester Airport.**

Be aware that some words may either be spelt differently in Britain and the USA, or may have different meanings, eg
- *airplane*
- *aluminum*
- *jelly*

In the box below, write down some words that describe your search. This might be single words or phrases, names of processes, people, organisations, places...

Begin by listing words and phrases which describe your topic as precisely as you can. Also think of words and phrases which relate, in some way, to your search. There may be different ways of expressing the topic using different words with the same or similar meanings. There may also be different spellings for your words.

Identify some strategies to help you, such as:

- **work with somebody else**
- **find a source of information which gives an explanation for your topic or provides an introduction to it (eg encyclopaedia, subject related dictionary, thesaurus)**
- **ask for advice from someone who already knows more than you about the subject or about searching for information.**

What strategies could you use to make your own search easier to do?

10.1.5 If things go wrong

Before you start using a computerised information resource – reflect on what you might do when things happen which you don't expect, or don't want. You could:

- press an **Escape** key, as a way back to where you were
- look for an option that says **Cancel**
- repeat what you did – this may cancel what you have done, or may help you to understand what happened
- ask for help from someone nearby – especially useful if what happened seems strange to you
- ask an expert
- use the **Help** facility
- make notes on what happened and what you did
- return later and try again.

> If you meet any problems, make a note of what you did to sort out a problem, what happened, and how you fixed it. This will help you think about similar problems in the future.

10.1.6 Deciding where to search

You should now be clearer about what you are looking for. The keywords you have identified may help you to decide where to look for information. You could also:

- look at course materials and reading lists
- ask for advice, either from an 'expert', or someone at the same stage of learning as you.

The task might involve retrieving information from:

- a computerised library catalogue, often known as an **OPAC (On-line Public Access Catalogue)**
- a general or specialised subject database
- the Internet
- a spreadsheet (display, manipulation and calculation of numbers on a computer)
- an electronic mail system (sending and receiving messages on a computer network).

A database is a collection of information which is organised to make it easier to find what you are looking for.

10.2 Carrying out your search

You will find it most useful to work through this section at a computer which has access to appropriate information sources. This may be at work or at college, or you may have a computer at home or at work which has suitable facilities, eg access to the Internet, CD-ROM encyclopaedias or databases. Make notes as you work through.

10.2.1 Searching

Look at the screen to see how to find the information resource of your choice. There are different ways of starting up computerised information resources. You may:

- **be able to select from a list or menu**
- **see pictures or symbols (known as *icons*) which represent an information resource to choose from**
- **type something in**
- **follow instructions**
- **explore.**

If you are not sure what to do, try out the various options, or ask for help.

Information resources work in a variety of ways. You need to get your chosen resource to a point at which you can start using it to look for information. You may need to use a button or menu item marked **Search, Query** or **Find,** for example.

Some ways of telling the information source what to look for include:

- **type in a word, words or phrases**

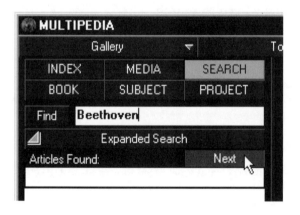

It is very important to read carefully the instructions, messages and warnings on each screen.

- **or type a letter or number,**

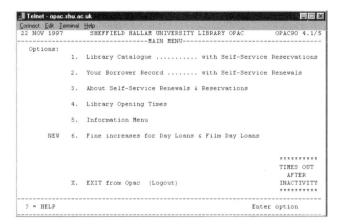

- **or select from a list,**

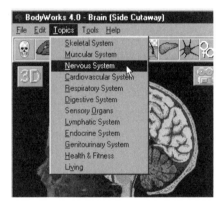

- **or a combination of these options.**

In some cases you will need to press a button or use a menu item to start the search.

If you are unsure what to type, different strategies you could try include:

- **test out different words and phrases**
- **look for instructions on the screen**
- **look for help on-screen**
- **use a self help guide**
- **experiment.**

NOTES

Searching can take some time. There may be an indication of progress or activity on the screen

You may recognise some common features/patterns to the way in which the information resource behaves which help you search in future. When searching an information resource, use the box below to make a note of what you see on-screen. Have a look at several screens.

10.2.2 More searching...

You may not get what you want straight away. Look at the screen to help you decide what to do next. You may need to:

- **follow further on-screen instructions**
- **repeat what you have already done**
- **answer some questions**
- **use on-screen help**
- **ask for advice**
- **try another service or resource, or another approach.**

Often you find the information in stages. The result of the first stage may be:

	Example
• **the piece of information you were looking for**	*the telephone number*
• **something telling you where to find the thing you want**	*the telephone directory is on the bottom shelf in aisle D*
• **the start of a new search**	*...of electronic Yellow Pages*

10.2.3 Evaluating what you find

It is important to look carefully at the results of your searches and to decide if you have found what you want. It may be that:

- **you have found part of the answer and you need to explore further to complete your task**
- **the answer may not exist, or may not exist in the form that you want**
- **you need to use a different approach in your search, or search elsewhere for the answer**
- **you have invested enough time already and further time spent in searching would not be justified.**

You also need to be critical about the results of your searches by assessing what they mean.

Once you have found the information you want, you should ask yourself questions about what you have found:

Are your results reasonable and do they make sense?

Do you need to search for more information on this topic (ie, do you actually have all that you need?)

How was the information gathered / created and by whom?

Do you need to do anything with the results in order to make use of what you've found?

10.3 Reflecting on your progress

You can complete this section once you have finished at the computer. It may help to look back over your notes in the chapter.

10.3.1 Developing your searching skills further

How might you develop your searching skills further? It may be helpful to:

- compare what you have done with someone else who is doing the same or a similar search
- identify other approaches to use for your search.

✔	Review what you have learnt to do so far.
	Plan and prepare a search
	Select suitable information resources to search
	Recognise how information resources are organised
	Select terms to search with
	Move around computerised information resources

Do you feel you have succeeded in what you tried to do? If so, what contributed most to the success?   What did you find difficult?

If you have identified something you find difficult, you could:

- try talking with someone who is at the same or similar stage as you but who is not finding those particular things difficult
- talk to an expert

or you may simply find it useful to take a break and come back later for another go.

11
WORKING
WITH SEVERAL
WINDOWS

This chapter takes you through the process of working with many windows open on the computer screen.

It aims to get you to a point where you can work on a single application such as a word processor with several documents at once, and where you can work with several different applications at once, such as a word processor, electronic mail and spreadsheet. What you learn using this chapter will be useful on any computer which allows you to work with multiple programs and with any application which allows you to open more than one document.

Before you start:

- you should already be able to use at least two different programs on your computer, for example the programs described in Chapters 4 to 10 of this book.

When you have completed this chapter, you will be able to:

- work with several documents open at once in a single application, for example in a word processor
- copy and paste between documents in a single application
- use more than one program on the computer at a time, for example a word processor and a spreadsheet
- copy and paste between documents in different programs
- monitor your own progress, identify successes and where you need to improve.

The skills that you develop with the aid of this chapter should help you to integrate the use of any programs that you already know how to use.

11.1 Background

You can read and think about this section away from the computer.

11.1.1 Doing several things at once

So far this book has concentrated on using a single application at a time (for example, a word processor) and has encouraged you to work on a single document at a time. However, the real power of the computer you are using becomes apparent only when you start working on more than one thing at a time.

In this chapter, you will start by learning to work with more than one document at a time, copying material from one document to another and switching between the documents. Later, you will also look at working with more than one application program and copying material from a document in one program to one in another.

Graphical computer systems (eg Windows, Macintosh) are designed to allow you to have several **windows** open at a time, providing you with a view of several things happening at once on the computer. So, for example, the screen below shows a word processor working on more than one document:

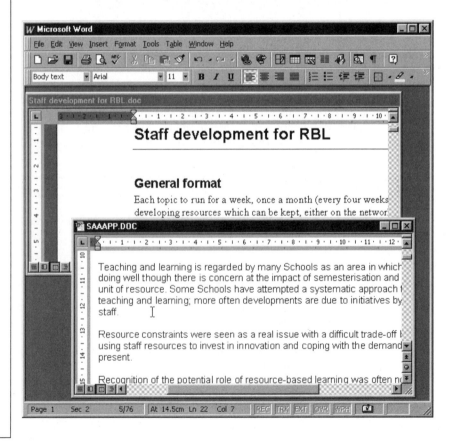

There are several things to notice about this picture:

- **the writer is working on two different documents, 'SAAAPP.DOC' and 'Staff development for RBL.doc'**
- **each document is in a separate window**
- **each window contains its own set of controls, like scroll bars**
- **the 'top' or 'front' window contains SAAAPP.DOC, and this is indicated by a different appearance of the bar at the top of the window**
- **the two document windows are contained in the program (or application) window, which has the title Microsoft Word.**

Working on two or more documents at once allows you to:

- **copy and paste material from one document to another**
- **use one document on screen as a reference while you work on another.**

Similarly, it is possible to work on more than one program at a time. The picture below shows a spreadsheet and a word processor in use at the same time:

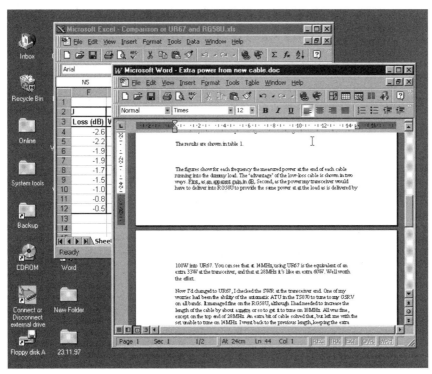

Here you have two windows, one for a word processor and one for a spreadsheet, with one document in each. The table in the spreadsheet is about to be pasted into the word processed document.

Part of the skill in working with more than one document, or with more than one application open at a time, lies in having your own understanding of how the windows behave on the screen, and knowing how to control them. The rest of this chapter will help you explore the way your own programs and computer manage windows on screen.

11.2 Opening several documents at once

You are going to start up an application program, for example a word processor, and open or create more than one document.

     Start an application program – for example, start your word processor.

Open one document, and notice where it is in the program window. In many cases, the document that you open will take up the whole of the space available in the application window, like this:

Unfortunately, some programs will not allow you to have more than one document open at a time. If this is the case, you will have to try this out with a different program.

Now try to open or start a new document. In most cases, the application will allow you to have the second document open at the same time as the first one.

Check that you actually do have two documents open at once. You may be able to:

*   **see both documents**
*   **find a list of documents, for example they may be listed on a Window menu.**

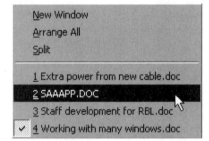

Find a list of documents, for example by looking on a **Window** menu. Try selecting each of the documents listed in the Window menu, and make a note here of what happens.

If you work on more than one document, make sure you save the changes to every document before you exit from the program.

NOTES

11.3 Changing the size of windows

You should now have an application program running with two (or more) documents open. What you are going to do in this section is explore ways in which your computer allows you to change the size of windows. You should make notes as you go along.

Much of the written material on changing the size of windows is likely to be in books, guides or help systems relating to the computer and the operating system, rather than those relating to individual programs.

11.3.1 Maximizing, minimizing and restoring

Depending on your own computer system, a window can have up to three different sizes:

maximized
when the window takes up the whole of the space available to it; for a document window in an application (eg in a word processor) the document will take up the whole space in the word processor window (see the picture on page 153)

minimized
when the window is reduced to a small representation, either an icon or a text item on some sort of task bar

normal, or restored
in this state, the window will be smaller than the whole space available to it; you can adjust the exact size to suit your needs (for example, both of the two documents shown in the picture on page 153).

 Work out whether the document window(s) you can see in your own application are:

* **maximized**
* **minimized**
* **normal.**

Depending on the state that your windows are in, you may need to go through the exercises below in a different order.

First, see how many different ways you can find of doing each of the following. The ways listed below may not all work on your computer; tick those that do.

To find out how to do these things, you may have to
• use the Help system on your computer
• refer to a manual or guide for your computer
• ask someone

NOTES

Maximizing a document window:

You could try :
*   clicking on a **Maximize** button, often on the top right of the window
*   finding a menu item to **Maximize** the window
*   double clicking on the bar at the top of the window
*   any other ways

From the maximized state, restoring the size to normal:

You could try :
*   clicking on a **Restore** button (often on the top right of the window)
*   finding a menu item to **Restore** the window
*   double clicking on the bar at the top of the window
*   moving the mouse to the edge or corner of the window, and dragging the edge of the window to the size that you want
*   any other ways

Minimizing a document window:

You could try :
*   clicking on a **Minimize** button (often on the top right of the window)
*   finding a menu item to **Minimize** the window
*   any other ways

From the minimized state, restoring the size to normal:

You could try :
*   clicking on a **Restore** button (often on the top right of the window)
*   finding a menu item to **Restore** the window
*   double clicking on the minimized representation (icon or text)
*   any other ways

From the minimized state, maximizing the window:

You could try :
*   finding a menu item to **Maximize** the window
*   any other ways

11.3.2 Changing the size of a window

You will probably be able to change the size of the document window by dragging one or more of the edges or corners. Sometimes, one or more of the corners may be marked to indicate that this is possible.

 Move the mouse to the side, top, bottom, or corner. In one or more of these positions, the cursor is likely to change as it moves over the edge of the window to indicate that you can now drag (ie **hold** the mouse button down and move the mouse) to resize the window. This may take some practice to do accurately.

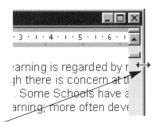

Frequently, the cursor changes to a double-headed arrow to indicate that you can resize the window.

Try it – make a note here of which of these positions allow you to resize the window:

- **Side**
- **Top**
- **Bottom**
- **Corner**

Note – although most windows will allow you to change their size, there are some windows that will not. You may also find that some windows cannot be reduced below a certain size.

11.4 Switching between windows

When you have several document windows open at once, one window sits 'on top' or 'in front' of another. The window at the front is described as the 'active' window, and is the one in which anything you do takes place. So, for example, if you have several documents open in a word processor, the one in the active window is where anything you type will appear; anything you do using menus or buttons will happen to the document in the active window.

In order to work with several documents, you have to be able to switch between different document windows. There are several ways of doing this, and which you use will depend both on your personal preference and on which is most suitable for the work you are doing.

You should try all the ways below to see which work with your program and your computer.

Selecting from a list of windows

On page 154, you tried selecting items from a list of windows. This way should be available on any program that you use with several documents open.

Clicking on another document window

If you click on one of the inactive document windows (ie one that is partially hidden behind the active window), it will become the active window. You can then work on that document. Try it.

Note here how your system indicates which is the active document window, and how this is different from the other document windows.

In order to click on an inactive document window, you may need to resize (see above) or move (see below) one or more other windows to make the inactive window visible.

Note – there may also be a menu item or button which allows you to arrange the document windows in different ways. This may simply offer the possibility to **Arrange** *the windows, or may offer the chance to* **Tile** *or* **Cascade** *the windows. You should try these options out to see what they do.*

11.5 Moving windows

With several windows open at once on the same screen, you may wish to move one window out of the way, so that you can see the window behind.

 Make sure that the active window is **not** maximised, ie make sure that it does **not** take up all of the space available to it. Try moving the active window by positioning the cursor over the top bar of the window, and then holding the mouse button down and **dragging** the active window to a new position.

*This will **not** work if the active document window is maximized.*

Search through the menus, the manuals, guide books or the help system for your computer to see if you can find another way of moving windows, and try it. Make a note here of how you did it.

As you move the window, you may see just a rectangular outline moving instead of the whole window.

11.6 Copying and pasting between documents

Just as you can copy material from one place in a document and place it somewhere else (see, for example, p 40), you can also copy material from one document that you have open and paste it into another document.

So, in the example here, the material highlighted in black might be copied from one document and pasted into the other document.

Try it:

- **select some text or other items in the active window**
- **copy what you have selected to the clipboard in the usual way (see p 40)**
- **make another window active, by clicking on it or selecting from a list of windows**
- **paste the selection from the clipboard into the new window.**

11.7 Closing windows

When you exit the application, it will close all the document windows. However, there will also be a number of ways of closing individual windows.

Explore the program on your own computer, and see which of the following are possible:

Clicking on a Close button on the top bar of the **document** (notice – this is similar to the button you use to close the application, but will be on the document window).

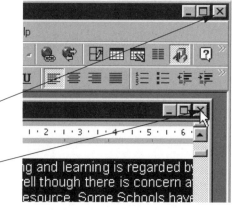

*The button on the top bar of the **application** closes the application program.*

*The button on the top bar of the **document** closes the document window.*

Finding a menu item (there may be more than one) to close the active document window.

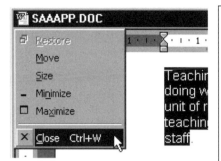

 As you close document windows, make sure you have saved each document. If you close the whole application program, you should make sure you have saved every document that you have open.

11.8 Working with more than one application

Just as you have worked with more than one document open in a single application, you can also work with more than one application open at a time. The principles are very similar to the way you work with multiple documents in a single application.

Somewhere on your computer screen there will be a way of obtaining a list of the open applications. Find out what this is and make a note here of how to do it.

Investigate on your computer with more than one application open at a time (for example, open a word processor and a spreadsheet). Make a note of how to do the following on your computer:

Maximize the application window
Minimize the application window
Restore the application window
Resize the application window
Move the application window
Bring an application window to the front
Copy material from a document in one application to a document in another application

The way you do these is likely to depend on the computer, and not on the individual application programs. When you use a different computer system, these may be similar, but you may need to explore again to find out how they work.

If you work with several applications open at once, it becomes even more important to shut the computer down in a proper, controlled way, so that all your work is safe. This is covered in more detail in Chapter 3 – **Beginning to Use a Computer.**

As you continue to use the computer, you will probably find that you become more expert in working with a number of documents open and switching back and forward between applications. So for example, at any one time you may have:

- **a word processor open as you work on a written document**
- **an email program open to send emails and read replies as they arrive**
- **a drawing program to produce diagrams to include in your document**
- **a file management program open to keep track of filed documents.**

Although you may only be able to see the active window or the active application, the other (background) windows are still busy, doing whatever they need to do to achieve their purpose. They will also take up some of the computer's resources (memory, for example), and so working with a large number of windows at once may make your computer run more slowly or even may mean that the computer puts some sort of error messages on the screen. If this happens, you may need to close some of the windows to get back to normal.

11.9 Reflecting on your progress

You can complete this section once you have finished at the computer. It may help to look back over your notes to the previous section.

✔	Tick what you have learnt to do.
	Maximize a window
	Minimize a window
	Restore a window
	Copy and paste between documents in a single application
	Resize a window by dragging one edge or a corner
	Bring a window to the front
	Copy and paste between documents in different applications

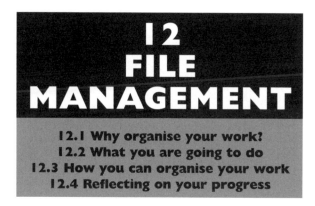

12
FILE
MANAGEMENT

12.1 Why organise your work?
12.2 What you are going to do
12.3 How you can organise your work
12.4 Reflecting on your progress

This chapter is a basic introduction to organising your work on computer disks.

It aims to help you understand how the work you produce on a computer is stored and how you could organise your work.

Before you start:

- you should understand the basic features of your computer, eg how to work with windows and a mouse. Earlier chapters in this book should help you to get to this point
- you should already know how to use applications such as word processors.

When you have completed this chapter, you will be able to:

- identify reasons for organising your work
- identify a structure in which to organise your work
- identify different disk drives
- create folders/directories
- identify and use file management tools to use to organise your work eg copy/move files and folders, rename files and folders, delete files and folders, find files and folders
- monitor your own progress, identify successes and where you need to improve.

What you learn in this chapter will help you to organise your own work on any personal computer using a graphical display (for example, running Windows).

NOTES

12.1 Why organise your work?

Here are some reasons why you might want to organise your work. Which of these apply to you?	✔
To find your work quickly and easily	
To see what work you have at a glance	
To store related pieces of work together	
To delete unwanted pieces of work on your disk	
To back up your work	
To give your work to someone else	
Others. Please add your own	

Here are two examples of ways you could organise your work on a disk. Which of them do you think would allow you to access your work more easily?

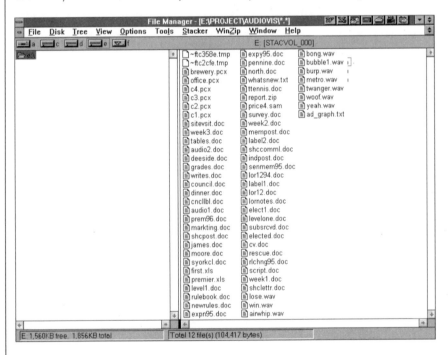

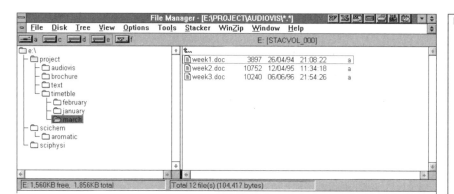

If you chose the second example you are thinking along the right lines.

How do you currently organise your work, eg alphabetically, by subject, not at all... ?	
Under what main headings could you organise your work?	What subheadings do you need under each main heading?

12.2 What you are going to do

You can read and think about this section away from the computer.

12.2.1 Learning computer skills

One of the most successful ways of learning to use a computer is to explore. In this chapter we help you to explore how to organise your work by managing your files effectively.

> *Be wary of simply copying down sequences of key presses or mouse clicks. It is much more effective to identify the general principles behind what you are doing. A copied sequence of actions may not work as you expect the next time you use it because the way the computer responds will also depend on other things such as what you were doing just before you carried out the actions.*

12.2.2 Identify a suitable task

Many people find it more effective to learn by carrying out a real task at the computer. This way you are likely to remember more effectively what you have learnt. The most obvious task that can be carried out in this chapter is to organise your work on a floppy disk. You need a disk with quite a few files on it, but use a disk that doesn't contain important work. Avoid the risk of taking on something too difficult or losing lots of important work. You could, for example, work on a copy of a disk that you normally use for your work.

Make notes here about your task.

12.3 How you can organise your work

To organise your work effectively you need to know a bit about where your work is stored.

Files

Each piece of work you produce on a computer is called a **file.** Files are either stored on the hard disk within the computer or on a floppy disk in the floppy disk drive. The secret of successfully organising your work is storing files in **folders** in a logical way, giving them names you can easily remember.

Disk Drives

Computer disk drives have names, rather in the same way that houses have numbers. This allows the computer and the person using the computer to identify which disk drive is going to be used. The names given to disk drives on an IBM PC-type computer follow the set of conventions shown below

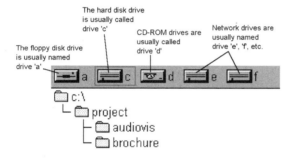

Other systems may use an icon to represent a disk drive or floppy disk. In these systems the disks and drives are often named by the person using them when they are used for the very first time, eg:

loan disk

Hard Disk

*A **floppy disk** contains a disc of flexible plastic which stores computer data. It is housed in a rigid plastic shell for support and protection.*

*A **folder** may also be called a **directory** or **subdirectory***

*A **disk drive** is a device that holds a disk, retrieves information from it, and stores information to it.*

A hard disk, or hard drive, is sealed in a case inside the computer. A hard disk can hold much more information than a floppy disk.

NOTES

In some systems, storage areas are called **directories** *and* **subdirectories**

In some systems the top level of the folder structure is called the **root.**

12.3.1 Storing files on disk

You can set up storage areas, called folders, in a structure on your disk. The top-level storage area on the disk can contain folders and files, and each folder, in turn, can contain other folders and files. In some systems the structure may be shown on its side, like this:

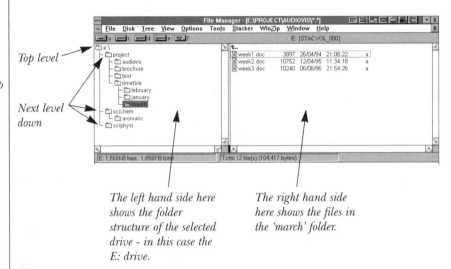

Top level

Next level down

The left hand side here shows the folder structure of the selected drive - in this case the E: drive.

The right hand side here shows the files in the 'march' folder.

Alternatively, your computer screen may look like this.

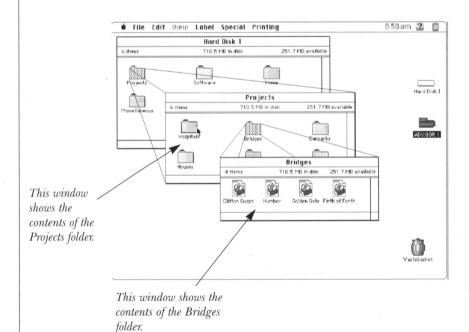

This window shows the contents of the Projects folder.

This window shows the contents of the Bridges folder.

Choosing names

When you create new files and folders you have to name them. Choose names that will help remember what an item is.

Some computer systems restrict your choice of names, for example they may :

- **limit you to using eight characters or fewer**
- **allow you to use only numbers and/or letters and/or some of the punctuation symbols**
- **forbid spaces in names.**

Filenames *on some computers frequently look like this:* **exercise.doc**. *The first part is the name you have given the file:* **exercise**. *The second part (***.doc***) is called the 'extension' and includes the dot followed by three characters. It is usually added by the computer and identifies the kind of information the file contains and which program created it. If you change the name of a file that has this type of filename, you must add the extension (including the dot) otherwise you may not be able to open the file.*

12.3.2 Floppy disks

It is useful to know what capacity your floppy disk is. A common capacity you may come across holds 1.44Mb of information. The disk itself can give you a clue to its capacity. 1.44Mb disks have two holes in the top corners, one of which has a sliding tab that may be pulled across, and usually have the letters HD on the front.

Write-Protect

You may want to protect the work on your disk so that it can't be altered or deleted but can still be read by the computer. If so, you should 'write-protect' the disk using the sliding tabs on the back of the disk.

When the tab is in the 'up' position (and you can see through the hole), the disk is write protected

When the tab is in the 'down' position you will be able to save new or altered files to the disk. You can move this tab up or down whenever you need to.

12.3.3 Organising your work with file management tools

In order to organise your work effectively, you will need to create a folder structure and move your files into the correct folders. File management 'tools' are used to do this work. You can **Copy, Move, Delete** and **Rename** files and folders as well as create new folders. There is usually some sort of Find File tool as well.

You will usually find the file management tools on your computer with the window that shows you your folders and files. This may be called something like **Finder, File Manager, Desktop** or **Explorer.** It may be the first window that appears when you start up, or you may be able to access it through a menu, button or icon from the first window.

What icon is associated with file management on your computer?		✔
Disk		
Disk Drive		
Filing Cabinet		
Folder		
Other / menu item		

The main things you will need to do to organise your work are:

- **create a folder structure**
  1. decide how you want to organise your work
  2. create each folder
  3. rename each folder, if necessary

- **move your files to appropriate folders.**

You will need to explore how to do these on your own computer. A lot of the things you need to do in order to organise your work may involve:

- **using commands on a File or Disk menu, or**
- **dragging icons from one place to another.**

Creating a new folder
You can create new folders at the top level of your disk, or within existing folders. If there are no folders on your disk, your new folder will be created at the top level. Otherwise, open the folder which will contain your new folder. Then look for an item on the **File** menu called **New**... or **Create**... Once the folder has been created, it will appear in the file management screen or window along with all the others. You will then be able to name or rename the new folder.

*Folder is another name for **directory** or **subdirectory***

Renaming a file or folder
Renaming a file or folder can be achieved on some computers by clicking in the name by the icon for the file or folder, then typing in a new name. Other computer systems may require the use of a menu item, usually on the **File** menu.

Click here to rename

Copying and moving files
You can copy or move a file from one place to a different disk or folder. When you copy or move items on a computer it is useful to be able to see the destination you want to copy or move to, as well as the item you want to copy or move, on screen at the same time. There may be a menu item called **Arrange All** or **Tile** on one of the menus, which will arrange open folders so that you can see them all at the same time on your screen. You may be able to copy or move more than one item at a time if they are in the same folder.

Deleting files and folders
You can remove unwanted files and folders by deleting them. Some file management windows have a 'recycling bin' or 'wastebasket' into which you can drag items for deletion. Other systems require the use of a **File** or **Disk** menu item or a key press to delete. When deleting a warning message may appear asking you to confirm your action.

Wastebasket

Lost files
When you create work you usually want to save it. If you have saved a file without telling the computer where you want to put it, you may wonder where it has gone. Don't panic – it will have been saved somewhere!

The place where your work will be saved will usually be either in a folder created by the program or on the floppy disk. One way of finding out where it has gone is to use the **Save As...** option in the program. The dialog box (see example below) which appears when you use **Save As...** will show the folder to which items are usually saved. Scroll down the list of work in the folder – your file should be there. Make a note of where it is so that you can move it later.

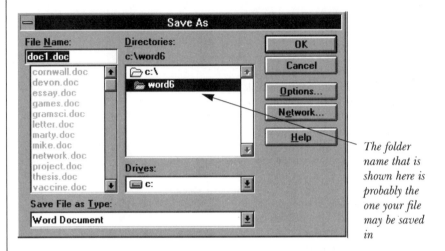

The folder name that is shown here is probably the one your file may be saved in

Search or Find File

You can also find missing files by using a **Search** or **Find File** option. This may be in a **File** or **Tools** menu. Most search systems will let you look for a file in different ways. You could search using the filename, the date the file was created or modified, or by type of file (eg word processing or graphic). You can even search for a file using a part of the file name, such as 'shc'.

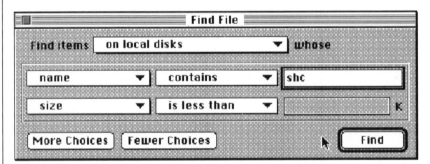

The example above will find files such as:

- shcollege.doc
- ashcliff
- cashclip.xls
- trishc

Accidentally deleted files

If you accidentally delete a file from your disk, it **may** be possible to recover it. Some computer systems have an **Undelete** function for files. You may wish to explore this *before* you need it.

You may be able to find a slightly earlier version of your work which you made as a backup yourself, or which was created automatically for you by the program which you were using. Such automatic backups sometimes have names which end in **.bak**. Your software manual may tell you whether your software does this kind of backup, and what it calls the files.

If you have deleted a **very** important file, it's probably best to get expert help because doing the wrong thing could make the file unrecoverable. As a general rule, if you need help in recovering a lost file you should leave the computer exactly as it was until you have contacted someone to help.

Wildcards

On some systems you can search for partial filenames using a ***** or **?** to substitute for the missing characters or character. These are known as **wildcards**. This is a special character that represents one or more other characters (numbers or letters) in the filename you are looking for.

You can use the **?** to represent any **single character,** and the asterisk ***** to represent any **character or group of characters** that might match that position in the name you are looking for. So if you were searching for a file called **shcdinnr.doc** but could not remember the **dinnr** bit you could search for **shc*.doc**.

For example:

- **her* means any name starting with her – her, here, heresy, herman**
- **b?n means any three letters starting with b and ending in n ; ban, bin, ben, bon, bun, bxn, bbn, bqn etc.**

NOTES

A backup is a copy of a file made to help with these problems. You can make backups yourself by simply copying files on to another disk or folder.

NOTES	How do you do the following on your computer?
	Copy files from folder to folder
	Copy files from disk to disk
	Move files from folder to folder
	Move files from disk to disk
	Delete files
	Rename files
	Find files

12.4 Reflecting on your progress

You can complete this section once you have finished at the computer. It may help if you look back over your notes.

✔ Review here what you have learnt so far.
Identify a structure for your work
Understand about disk drives
Copy files and folders
Delete files and folders
Rename files and folders
Create a new folder
Find lost files

> Do you feel you have succeeded in what you tried to learn? If so, what aspects of the way you worked contributed most to the success?
>
> What, in particular, did you find difficult?

If you have identified some aspects of file management which you find difficult, you could:

- **try talking with someone else who is at about the same level as you but who is not finding those particular things difficult**
- **talk to an expert**
- **visit a helpdesk or contact a support service**

or you may simply find it useful to take a break and come back another time to have another go.

13
LAYOUT AND STYLE

13.1 Background
13.2 Breaking down the task
13.3 Layout
13.4 Producing your design
13.5 Reflecting on your progress

This chapter is an introduction to laying out text on a computer.

It is designed to cover the use of word processors or desktop publishing programs to produce documents (if you are unsure whether to use word-processing or desktop publishing software, see page 184.) The principles you learn will also be relevant to other computer applications which you may use to present information – eg presentation graphics applications.

Before you start:

- you should already have some experience in using a word processor. You are likely to have reached this point if you have already worked through Chapter 4 – *Writing*, and Chapter 5 – *Making Tables*, and have spent some time exploring your word processor.

When you have completed this chapter, you will be able to:

- identify features of style, layout and page design, and analyse the effectiveness of those features in improving the appearance and impact of work
- identify ways in which you might improve the appearance of your own work
- analyse the requirements of your work and what would be appropriate to improve the appearance
- identify the meaning of particular computer terms
- design a layout for your work, including text and graphics where appropriate
- implement your design at the computer
- print your work accurately
- monitor your own progress, identify successes and where you need to improve.

What you learn in this chapter will be relevant to working with word processors and desktop publishing programs on any personal computer using a graphical display (for example, running Windows).

13.1 Background

You can read and think about this section away from the computer.

13.1.1 Why bother with improving the appearance of your work?

Although the content of what you write is often the most important factor, the impact and effect that your work will have depend also on the layout.

If you are producing a piece of work for course assessment, the assessment instructions may explicitly mention layout, but even if they don't the effect of good layout will make the work easier and more enjoyable to read, and that can have a significant effect on the marking.

Producing a well laid-out piece of work may be more satisfying, and a good, well-presented project or application can help you in job interviews.

13.1.2 Identify a suitable task

Many people find it more effective to learn by carrying out a real task at the computer. However, practising on a task which is complex, large, or urgent may put pressure on you and could prevent you from learning thoroughly. Identify a task that allows you to practise and learn without the risk of your taking on something too difficult.

A suitable task may involve producing a piece of written work:

• **from one to several pages long**
• **in which a good layout might help the understanding or the readability of the work**
• **which is well structured.**

Examples include:

• **a report or essay of several pages**
• **a piece of promotional material**
• **an article for a newsletter or a magazine.**

Write a brief outline here of what you will use as your task:

13.1.3 Look at similar examples

Graphic artists, magazine designers, and desktop publishers often start a design by looking at examples of similar existing documents in order to:

- **gather new ideas**
- **look at a range of ways of laying out the material**
- **free their minds of any preconceptions that might hinder the production of a good design.**

It is a good idea to look at other documents **before** you have your own ideas about layout. Because form and content are often closely linked, you might also want to look at other documents for ideas before you even start writing the text.

Gather together some examples of work similar to what you want to produce. These may not be exactly the same as your task, but you are looking for something broadly similar, eg:

- **similar work done by others, for example projects done by students in a previous year**
- **model answers**
- **magazine and newspaper articles**
- **book chapters**

that deal with the same *type* of information.

Look carefully at each example and make brief comments using the following headings:

- **purpose** – *what is the document for?*
- **overall impression** – *what effect does it achieve?*
- **audience analysis** – *who is it aimed at?*
- **rules and conventions** – *what are the constraints you will be working under? eg does your tutor or subject have any particular requirements?*
- **chunking** – *how is the information broken down into manageable chunks?*
- **signposting** – *how does the reader find their way through the information?*
- **success** – *what makes this example good or bad?*

Rules and conventions
These may include course regulations, as well as less formal conventions. Check the course documentation to ensure that your design meets the requirements of the course assessment. Eg many courses insist you produce dissertations double-spaced.

NOTES

If you need more information about these headings, you should look at the chapters on **Essay Writing** and **Report Writing** in *The Student Skills Guide,* by Sue Drew and Rosie Bingham.

Think of some words to describe the overall impression you get from the layout of each of the examples you have chosen. Are they:

- **exciting?**
- **dull?**
- **serious?**
- **lighthearted?**

You could also make some notes about how they have achieved this impression. What about each example contributes to the overall effect you have identified?

13.1.4 Start thinking about your own document

Now that you have some ideas about what sort of layout might help your work, make notes here about your own task:

Intended purpose – *what is your document for?*

Intended impression – *what effects do you want your document to have (eg serious / scholarly / exciting / modern)?*

Audience analysis – *who is your document aimed at? What do you know about this audience?*

Rules and standards – *are there any relevant regulations, or conventions, that you must or might follow?*

Chunking – *how can you break the information down into manageable chunks?*

Signposting – *how does the reader find their way through the information?*

Criteria for success – *what are the characteristics of a 'good' and successful document?*

Purpose
You could think about two aspects :
1. why you are producing this document (eg to get a mark, to learn about something, etc)
2. what role is the document intended to play (eg as a report to a managing director, as a newspaper article, etc).

In designing the document, meeting purpose (2) may well help you achieve purpose (1).

13.1.5 Plan your work

Consider the layout and presentation of your work at an early stage. Producing well-presented work takes some time, and you should allow for this.

> How much time do you intend to spend on each of the following parts of your document:
>
> • **planning**
>
> • **writing**
>
> • **inputting information (eg typing)**
>
> • **formatting**

Beware of spending excessive amounts of time producing an outstanding layout – you should try to gauge what will be 'good enough' for what you need.

13.1.6 Word-processor or desktop publisher?

A few years ago, it was easy to explain the difference between word-processing and desktop publishing software. Word-processing programs were originally good for editing text but not very flexible in terms of page design; desktop publishing programs offered flexible page design, but were not good for editing text.

Recently, word-processor software has 'borrowed' features from desktop publishing and vice versa. The original SkillPacks on which this book was based were prepared using word-processor software, although they contain quite a few graphics and some quite complicated page design. It is worth looking at both types of program so you can see how they work in practice.

As a general rule of thumb, we suggest that:

• **you use a word-processor if the page design is fairly simple, especially if it is a long, continuous document**
• **you choose a desktop publisher if the page design is very complicated or broken up, with a lot of graphics or illustrations.**

13.2 Breaking down the task

It is often easier to appreciate the design of a well-presented document by thinking about three overlapping but clearly recognisable aspects of design – structure, style and layout.

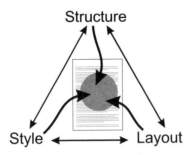

The next section will deal with layout in some detail, but first we will look briefly at structure and style.

*Structure and style are dealt with more fully in the chapters on **Essay Writing** and **Report Writing** in **The Student Skills Guide,** by Sue Drew and Rosie Bingham.*

13.2.1 Structure

Every document has a structure – this is the way that the content of the document is organised and split up so that it is clear for the reader. One way of signalling the structure of the document to the reader is to use headings and subheadings. The structure of a document will give it a distinctive appearance.

How would you structure a report on a work experience placement? What headings and sub-headings would you use to divide it into sections?

You could structure it:

- **chronologically, with headings of the weeks or months in order**

- **by themes, so the headings could be main features of the placement, like:**
  Introduction to the placement
  How the organisation worked
  How my work was organised and managed
  What I achieved

- **by what you learned – the main things that you got out of the placement:**
  How my technical skills developed
  What I learned about the organisation
  How I developed relationships with people at the placement.

If you were the course tutor marking all of these reports, which structure would you think was the most useful of these?

The structure of the document you are producing may give you clues to the layout you might adopt.

It is worth investigating whether your program can help you define the structure of your work even before you start writing anything. For example:

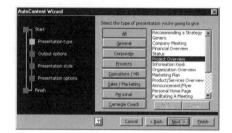

- **many word processors incorporate some sort of *outliner***
- **some presentation graphics packages will suggest typical structures for common presentation tasks - eg, presenting a report.**

Outline the sort of structure you expect your document to have. Don't worry about detail – just indicate headings and order.

13.2.2 Style

It is important to make sure that the style you choose *works* for the task you are doing. The elements of style that you choose should at least be appropriate to the task - eg, you may need to be cautious in the use of humour. (See the chapters on **Essay Writing** and **Report Writing** in *The Student Skills Guide,* by Sue Drew and Rosie Bingham.)

Many computer programs for writing can help with some aspects of style, eg word processors may offer help with grammar and spelling. Be careful though – any corrections the program offers may not always be appropriate, and even if the program says that your work is correctly written, you should still check it for typographical errors (including spelling mistakes, punctuation errors and typing errors) and grammatical mistakes.

 Get a feel for how your spelling checker works and how it fits with your way of writing. Some of the things which it may not be able to deal with are:

- **names of people (what does it suggest as 'correct' spellings?)**
- **right words in the wrong place or context (eg using 'there' when 'their' is needed)**
- **obscure or technical words spelt wrongly**
- **US / British English spelling (eg 'color' and 'colour')**
- **alternative spellings (eg 'organise' and 'organize')**
- **hyphenated words (eg 'co-operate').**

You could also try out a grammar checker with, for example:

- **something grammatically correct but meaningless, like**
  Colourless green ideas sleep furiously
- **spoken language, which tends to be very different from writing.**

Many aspects of grammar and spelling checkers can be turned off or adjusted.

NOTES

Style *means at least three different things. In this section, we use the term style in relation to content and the way you write, where it means things like*
• *language level (eg simple or complex vocabulary, sentence structure...)*
• *approach to the topic*
• *your choice of words*
• *grammar*
• *the use of humour.*

On a computer it means, specifically, either the bold, italic etc nature of text **or** *a record of all the formatting information about a paragraph or word or for later use (see page 196).*

13.3 Layout

The 'layout' is the way a document is laid out on the paper or computer screen. These three documents have distinct layouts, which reflect their purpose and use:

One long piece of writing, with headings and paragraphs all related to a single topic and forming a single sequence

A newsletter, with separate stories on different topics mixed with pictures and headlines

A folded leaflet, with separte pieces of information on related topics, mixed with pictures

You may find good ideas for layout in:

- **closely related documents – eg the work done by students on the course last year**
- **very different documents doing the same function – eg magazine articles or sales brochures.**

The next section defines some of the words you'll come across when you start to work on your page layout.

13.3.1 Layout glossary

Running heads

Items which appear on every page, normally at the top (the header) or bottom (the footer) of the page. The header at the top of this page includes the page number, generated automatically by the word-processor, and the chapter title.

Headings and subheadings

Section headings, usually formatted differently from the rest of the text, in typeface, position or both. On this page, '**13.3.1 Layout glossary**' is a subheading.

Margins

The lines (not printed) which define the area on the page where the work appears.

Alignment

Where the text lines up – against the left-hand margin, the right-hand margin or centred between the margins. Normally the text lines up straight at the side it is aligned to and is ragged at the other side, like this paragraph. If you ask for the text to be *flush* or *justified*, the software will add extra spaces to line it up straight at both sides.

margins

page

margins

Indent

How far a paragraph is offset from the margin. This paragraph is indented about half a centimetre more from the left than the word 'Indent' above.

Bullets and numbering

Simple signposting for lists – eg see the bulleted lists throughout section 13.1.3.

White space

Text is easier to read if it's not just a solid mass of text. White space is the name for areas on the page deliberately left blank to help the reader.

Rules

Horizontal or vertical lines which help to define the layout.

Columns

Vertical columns of text, as in a newspaper.

Font

Font name (also called typeface) eg Arial, Times, *BrushScript*. ⋯✂⋯

Style   eg normal **bold** *italic* ***bold-italic*** <u>underlined</u>

Size   eg 12 point, 18 point, 24 point

Text size is often measured in points - a point is 1/72nd of an inch. 12 point is a commonly used size.

NOTES

*Paper
orientation -*

*portrait
or*

landscape

13.3.2 Analysing page layout

These diagrams show some of the components of document layout. There are obviously many more, but this at least gives you an idea of some of the things you may need to think about in laying out your document.

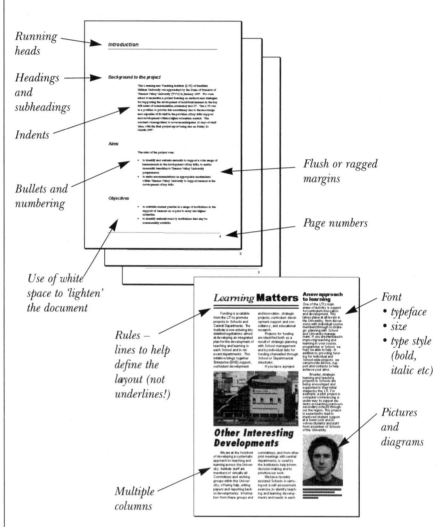

Running heads

Headings and subheadings

Indents

Bullets and numbering

Use of white space to 'lighten' the document

Rules – lines to help define the layout (not underlines!)

Multiple columns

Flush or ragged margins

Page numbers

Font
- *typeface*
- *size*
- *type style (bold, italic etc)*

Pictures and diagrams

Look at some examples of documents like the one you want to produce. List the main layout features that they use to achieve their intended effect. Which of these might you use in your document?

NOTES

13.3.3 Achieving consistent page design

One feature which helps documents look 'professional' is the use of a consistent page design. This means that the following features are used consistently throughout the document:

- **margins**
- **header**
- **footer**
- **page numbers**
- **use of columns (if you need them).**

See page 189 for an explanation of these terms.

Your software can help you here, as most word-processor and desktop publishing programs have one or more boxes which show you what these settings are and allow you to adjust them eg:

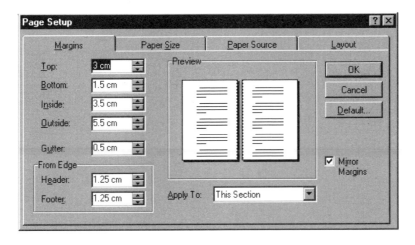

Decide on what measurements you want to use and enter them in the table below. You might get a better idea of what measurements you want if you draw a sketch of the page on a full sheet of paper.

	what you want for your document
Top margin	
Bottom margin	
Left margin	
Right margin	
Header (eg. title of document)	
Footer (eg. page numbers)	
Page numbers	
Use of columns	

Find out how to adjust these in your word-processor; eg you might look for a menu item called something like **Page Setup, Print Setup,** or **Document.**

13.3.5 Design details

There are many books explaining the basic principles of graphic design that you can consult for different ideas and approaches. It is also worth considering some of the following specific guidelines which graphic designers use to make documents look 'professional'.

Only use a limited number of fonts or typefaces
Your computer will offer you a variety of fonts, including the following, or ones which are very similar:

* Times, which is a 'serif' typeface because it has serifs, the small decorative squiggles at the ends of the individual letters
* Arial or Helvetica, which are 'sans-serif' typefaces as they have no serifs

See page 189 for an explanation of any unfamiliar terms.

A common combination is to use a serif typeface for the main text, and a sans-serif typeface for headings, and sub-headings. This book is written in Times New Roman (serif typeface), with Arial (sans-serif typeface) headings.

Try printing out a few lines in different typefaces and sizes to see which font looks right for your project.

Don't make lines of main text too long
Graphic designers recommend lines not less than 8 and no more than 20 words wide.

Use one space after a full stop
If you were taught to type, you may have been taught to leave two spaces after a full stop. This was a useful rule on typewriters, which used a font where all the characters had the same width. But word-processors and desktop publishing software use fonts in which different letters are different widths so your work looks best with a single space after each full stop.

Don't use the underline type style
Try using italics or bold text instead. You will find it usually looks better than underlining which tends to chop off the tails of the letters.

Use an indent or a blank line between paragraphs – but not both
Either will do but be consistent. Using both can leave too many white 'holes' on the page.

Avoid putting text in capitals, except for very short headings
Readers find long sentences in capitals off-putting and hard to read. Most graphic designers only use all-capitals on very short headings.

NOTES

Look at an example of a document which is the sort you want to produce. How many guidelines you can work out from it? Did it use any of the guidelines listed above?

Make a sketch here of how you intend your document to look. You do not have to write the text in – just use lines and blocks to give the effect.

13.3.6 Using visual aids

Using diagrams and illustrations can make a document look more interesting and professional, but be careful not to waste time with them. Consider using visual material when the following apply:

* you have ideas which will have more impact or be easier to understand if expressed visually, eg using a graph to show trends in information
* you have ideas which are difficult to express in words but can be done visually, eg using an organisation chart to show people's roles and relationships.

Use the following table to make notes on the visual aids you need for your document:

What idea do you want to express ?	What visual aid can you use? eg chart, graph, photo etc	What will the reader gain from this visual aid?

13.4 Producing your design

You will find it most useful to work through this section at the computer and to make notes as you work through.

Once you have an idea of how you want your document to look, you can start to produce it on the computer. You may be using a word processing program, or desktop publishing program.

13.4.1 Using styles on the computer

Most word processors and desktop publishing programs provide various ways of making it easier to produce well laid-out documents.

You can set up standard combinations of character and paragraph formatting, usually called *styles,* which you can apply either to a block of existing text or to text as you type it in – see the box below. The styles used in producing this page have been marked in the left margin.

Usually, a word processor or desktop publishing package comes with a number of standard built-in styles, but you can also define your own.

Find out how to apply built-in styles to text in your program. You may be able to choose a style first and then start typing, or type some text, select it, and then apply a style to it.

Look in a **Format** menu, or look for a drop-down list of styles to choose from.

Make and print out a **style sheet** – type a couple of lines of text (eg the alphabet, some numbers, and a few words) in some of the different styles available in your program. Choose which styles you would like to use in your document.

Collections of built-in styles may be held together in standard documents called **templates.** You may well have a number of different templates available for different jobs – eg, reports, essays, letters, etc. Sometimes templates also contain standard content – eg, the return address on a letter. When you start a new document, you may be given the choice of which template you'd like to use, or you may be able to 'attach' a template to a document you're working on. Look in a **File** or **Tools** menu or in the Help for your software.

Normal: abcdefghijklmnopqrstuvwxyz ABCDEFGHIJKLMNOPQRSTUVWXYZ 1234567890 The quick brown fox jumps over the lazy dog

Body text: abcdefghijklmnopqrstuvwxyz ABCDEFGHIJKLMNOPQRSTUVWXYZ 1234567890 The quick brown fox jumps over the lazy dog

Heading 1: abcdefghijklmnopqrstuvwxyz
ABCDEFGHIJKLMNOPQRSTUVWXYZ
1234567890 The quick brown fox jumps over the lazy dog

Heading 2: abcdefghijklmnopqrstuvwxyz
ABCDEFGHIJKLMNOPQRSTUVWXYZ 1234567890 The quick brown fox jumps over the lazy dog

Heading 3: abcdefghijklmnopqrstuvwxyz
ABCDEFGHIJKLMNOPQRSTUVWXYZ 1234567890 The quick brown fox jumps over the lazy dog

Body indent: abcdefghijklmnopqrstuvwxyz ABCDEFGHIJKLMNOPQRSTUVWXYZ 1234567890 The quick brown fox jumps over the lazy dog

13.4.2 Defining your own styles

As well as using the built-in styles, you may want to define your own styles.

Find out how to define your own styles. Try looking at the help system, or the manual, or explore the menus, especially a **Format** menu if there is one.

There are two main ways of defining your own styles:

- **by filling in forms on screen to set up the font, size, indent etc**
- **by example, where you set the font and paragraph up the way you want and then 'record' this as a new style.**

Find out which way your program works.

When you are setting up your own styles, it may be easiest to start with an existing style, modify it and save it with a new name. Change one thing at a time and see the effect of what you have done before making more changes, as you can usually **Undo** single changes.

Make a list here of the main features you intend to use in your document, and the styles you want to use – write the names of the styles, or if you are designing your own styles give more detail of each style

Feature	Style name	Typeface	Size	Character Style
Section titles (example)	*Heading 1*	*Times*	*18pt*	*Bold, Italic*

13.4.3 Printing your work

With most word processors and desktop publishing programs what you see on the screen is pretty close to what you see in the final printed document, but some of the problems you might meet include:

- **sometimes, your choice of printer may affect the position of text on the page, changing where new lines start or even where new pages start**
- **some of the fonts may not be available on the printer you use**
- **the fonts you use on one computer (eg at home) may not be available on the computer you use elsewhere (eg at work, college or university)**
- **if you want to send a copy of the document to someone else on disk or via email, check that the layout still works at the receiving end.**

Things you can try to avoid or correct these problems include:

NOTES

- set up the program at the start for the printer which you're going to use for the final print of your work
- use a **Print Preview** if your program has one, to see the appearance of the document before printing. Look on the menus for it – it's often near the **Print** command on the **File** menu
- print a test page *early on* so that you can iron out any problems before you hit your deadline
- check *early on* that any documents you send by email will work – try sending a short document as a sample and ask the receiver if it comes out all right
- if you will be using different computers to work on your document, limit the typefaces you use to those that will be available on the computer and printer that the document is going to end up on.

13.5 Reflecting on your progress

You can complete this section once you have finished at the computer. It may help to look back over your notes to the previous section.

✔ Review what you have learnt to do so far.
Choose appropriate structure, layout and style for your work
Apply built-in styles to headings etc
Create your own styles

Do you feel you have succeeded in what you tried to do? If so, what contributed most to the success?

What did you find difficult?

If you have identified something you find difficult, you could:

- **talk to another person who is at about the same level of learning as you but who is not finding those particular things difficult**
- **talk to an expert**
- **consult a helpdesk or support service**

or you may simply find it useful to take a break and come back another time and have another go.

Are you happy with what you have produced? Could it be better? To help you decide what you want to learn about next, look at more documents in newspapers, journals or books. Are there any other features that you would like to incorporate in your work? Explore the features of your program to see what it's capable of.